Concerned Parents --

You Can Help Your Public School

by Linden Boggs
with Joseph D. Allison

illustrated by Don Stuart

Library of Congress Cataloging-in-Publication Data:

Boggs, Linden.
  Concerned parents—you can help your public school.

  1. Public schools—United States. 2. Home and school—United
States. 3. Education (Christian Theology) I. Allison, Joseph
D. II. Title.
LA217.B64 1986   371'.01'0973   85-31926
ISBN 0-87403-080-3

Published by The STANDARD PUBLISHING Company, Cincinnati, Ohio.
A division of STANDEX INTERNATIONAL Corporation.
Printed in the U.S.A.

CONTENTS

INTRODUCTION

Do you have questions concerning your children and the public schools? Some parents question whether or not their children should attend public school. This choice of Christian school versus public school can be made by you only, the parents, after careful investigation, consideration, and prayer.

If you are a Christian parent, and you already know that your children will attend public schools either of necessity or by choice, you are probably asking many of the same questions as other Christian parents.

Some of your concerns may be:

- How may I help my child to have a positive learning experience if the school seems to have problems? What if there is conflict with the teacher? Is my child emotionally and educationally doomed?
- Why should I volunteer as an unpaid aide at my child's school? How may I bring it about if the school has no structured volunteer program?
- Is it possible for a single individual to have any kind of impact upon the school board and other policymaking bodies within the school system?
- What can I do to get acquainted with the staff, especially my child's teacher, if the school is large?
- Is it possible for me to know what is being taught in my child's classes if he is not allowed to bring some of the books home?
- My school teaches a sex education course. Should I allow my child to take it, and how do I decide? Can I see the instructional materials before the class is taught?
- What can I do if my child brings home an offensive textbook or material from the school library?

- Is there a right way and a wrong way to approach a teacher or administrator when I think something is wrong and ought to be changed?

These questions and many more must be answered in the minds of many parents before they can have confidence in the type of educational experiences their children are having in schools. At the same time, we must realize that most public schools have children from Christian homes. Many of these children are able to thrive spiritually and educationally in this environment with strong and close parental contact and support.

On some occasions, I have heard Christians lament the fact that many of our great social and governmental institutions are under the control of the world. Some of these institutions are described as being openly hostile to the Christian community as a whole.

At this point in our history as a nation and as members of the body of Christ, we must ask ourselves a question and answer it honestly. *Has our influence upon these institutions as Christians been wrenched from our grasp, or have we willingly and voluntarily forfeited our responsibilities and left a vacuum for others to fill?*

Why do we find so few Christians involved in the civil and social affairs of their communities? Are we too busy pursuing our own worldly pleasures? Do we find it too comfortable to associate only with the "company of the committed"? Maybe we simply seek to avoid any areas of potential conflict and unpleasantness. After all, didn't the apostle Paul strive to "live peaceably with all men"?

The church has been characterized as a sleeping giant. If this great force should awaken, what an impact it would have upon the world.

This book deals with only one small part of American society, but an important one, the schools. It is important because the public schools have some impact upon nearly ninety percent of the children in America. It is a small part because these children spend only about ten percent of their lives from birth until high school graduation in and around the school environment.

I have not attempted to write a scholarly appraisal of American public schools. The intent is to provide a primer of information and ideas for constructive involvement in those schools.

Christian schools are being started at the rate of several per week. While this may be good for the children who attend them, what about the other eighty-five or ninety percent of American children who attend public schools? Are they to be left alone with no input from the Christian community? As schools have become larger, they have seemed to also become more removed from the mainstream of the life of the communities they serve. As the doors are closed on small neighborhood schools, the students are nearly always combined with other students to form larger and "better" schools. These larger schools are more difficult "to get to know."

Many small neighborhood schools, with only one section of each grade level, will have mothers and sometimes fathers coming into the building each week to "help out." These parents know the principal, the secretary, all of the teachers, and many or most of the students. The parents often find this to be a familiar and comfortable situation.

The larger elementary school is becoming more common. It will often have five hundred or more students, and as many as twenty-five or more teachers. This alone is enough to create a psychological barrier between the school and parents. Parent contact with the school may be reduced, and separation between the school and home is enlarged. Parents may no longer feel as though they are on their own "turf." Their thinking may even change from "our school" to "that school."

Most of this can be overcome, but it won't often happen on its own. More deliberate effort is required, and it will take more time to feel comfortable in a large school. Some parents are simply unwilling to make the attempt.

You will become familiar with your school because you intend to become familiar with your school. You will know your child's teacher because you intend to. You will talk to the principal because you intend to. You will influence school board policy because you intend to. And you will be able to talk to your child about his school because you have been involved. Parents go to jobs. Children go to school. If you and your child both are involved in the school, you then have some common ground. Parents should take advantage of this whenever possible, because it is difficult to find common ground with our children in a world that is changing so rapidly.

The Christian parents I know have fears about their own children and what they will become. For more than two decades, I have watched as students have passed through their junior and senior high years. With very few exceptions, I have observed that the children of schoolteachers have done very well. Why? Is it because their parents were smarter than other parents? Certainly not! I believe it is because the parent and the child understand each other because they both do the same thing—they "do" school.

Very few schools are all good or all bad, though it's not hard to find staunch supporters or severe critics who feel otherwise. I believe that all schools, however good or bad, can be improved by strong parent involvement.

While many of us do not feel comfortable with change, we will nevertheless find that it will remain with us. There will always be more questions asked about schools and education than there will be answers provided.

Be True
to Your School

Consider this description of a public high school: It's a place where the Fellowship of Christian Athletes has 135 active members and several Christian faculty sponsors. It's a place where more than sixty students gather each Wednesday morning before classes begin for prayer and Bible study. This is led by a local youth minister. It's a place where students have formed a group that has been singing, sharing, and witnessing in local churches for the past twelve years. Or consider another public high school: It's a place where the principal forbids teaching of the Bible as literature. It's a place where Christian teachers are uneasy about sharing their convictions because parents don't seem to care. It's a place where students wrestling with sexual immorality, drug abuse, and a host of other problems must "go it alone," because school officials don't want to admit these problems exist in their school.

The schools I've just described are not hypothetical. They are real schools located in adjacent school districts, just sixteen miles apart. They are different largely because parents' involvement is different.

Christian parents care about what is happening in our public schools, and for good reason: Of the forty-three million students enrolled in elementary and secondary schools in this country, about thirty-eight million (or eighty-eight percent) are enrolled in public schools. Despite the hue and cry for more private schools, and the debate about tuition tax credits for private schools, *most Christian parents still send their children to public schools.* So Christian parents still have a big investment in the pubic schools. That's where their children do most of their formal learning; and that's where many of young people's values are shaped.

Do public schools have the power to make genuine changes in their students' social, moral, and spiritual development? If so ...

Do you feel your public school is having a destructive influence on your child's development? If it is ...

Do you have a duty to guide the influence that the school exerts upon your child?

I believe public schools *do* influence students' behavior. I have come to this conclusion after working in the public schools for more than twenty years as a school teacher, guidance counselor, and administrator. I have found that all of our schools influence the students under their care, just as all children are products of the homes in which they live.

Parents hear disturbing reports of drug abuse, vandalism, and violence (such as 70,000 teachers being assaulted each year). But not all of the news about our public schools is bad. In fact, some beautiful things are happening in our schools.

American educators have long dreamed that we could build a society of educated people. Every year we come closer to realizing that dream. *The American School Board Journal* reports[1] that in 1950 less than fifty percent of the students in this country were graduating from high school, while in 1977 over eighty percent finished high school. Less than ten percent of black students graduated from high school in 1950, while in 1977 at least seventy-six percent graduated.

Cynics would say, "Yes, more young people are graduating. It's just easier for them to get a diploma!"

Not really. The same article in *The American School Board Journal*[2] went on to share this information:

- —In 1900, 11.3 percent of the United States population was illiterate; in 1970, only 1.2 percent was illiterate (according to the Education Commission of the United States).
- —The reading test scores of fourteen-year-old students in the United States are consistently higher than the scores of students the same age in the Netherlands, Sweden, and the United Kingdom.
- —From 1975 to 1979, the number of books and periodicals borrowed from public libraries in the United States increased from 107 million to 123 million.

I could give you many more statistics, but I think these are enough to make my point: The educational standards of American public schools are *not* declining. They are rising. A recent test administered in California gave surprising proof of it. The standard tenth-grade competency exam was given to 120 adults from the local community (fifty-one percent of whom had college degrees). In each of the areas measured by the test—reading, writing, and arithmetic skills—current tenth graders scored *higher* than the adults![3]

So the dream of public education in America is coming true. Our children are getting a good education in the basic skills. We should commend our school officials for what they are doing in this respect. Our public schools provide a superior education at a minimal cost.

They are effective training centers for the future leaders of our nation, and of the world. Why dismantle the public school system just because it has flaws? Every institution does. But I believe the flaws in our school system challenge us to improve the system. They challenge all parents to get involved in the education of their children.

As our society's ills have increased, government leaders have tried to use our public schools to correct them. For example, the United States military found that many of its recruits for World War II were physically unfit because they had such poor diets. Solution? A push for the national school lunch program. State governments and insurance companies decried the increasing auto accident rate. Solution? We began driver's education programs. Health officials cried out against the rise in venereal disease and unwanted pregnancies among teenagers. Solution? We began sex education programs. These school programs have been an asset to our young people in many ways; certainly they have been needed. But imagine the heavy burden these programs place upon the public school system, which was started to teach the basic "three R's" of reading, 'riting, and 'rithmetic!

Not all of these attempts to correct social ills have been successful, either. I once heard a pastor compare our school system to a fabled little village on a mountaintop. The village children liked to play in a nearby field, but many of them fell from a cliff at the edge of the field and were killed. So the town fathers applied for a government loan of three million dollars to correct the problem. How? By building a hospital at the base of the cliff! The hospital did help, of course, but many children still died. So the town officials applied for more money to buy a shiny new ambulance to help the doctors give emergency aid. This helped the situation, too, but not enough. So the officials applied for yet *more* money to buy a fireman's safety net. They employed three shifts of rescue workers to stand at the base of the cliff and catch the children as they fell off. On a good day, they could catch three out of five.

We often try to address the *symptoms* of our social problems—as did the little village on the mountaintop—without addressing the *cause* of these problems. Why? Because we do not recognize the cause. Even though our coinage bears the motto, "In God We Trust," we live in a secular society. We are not able to understand the root cause of the moral and social problems that face us today. But we ardently hope our schools can train the next generation to avoid these problems.

The Bible says these problems spring from sin. Sin can manifest itself in many different ways. Every moral and social problem is rooted in sin. Virtually every moral and social problem that bubbles to the top of our society will surface in the public schools. And that's where we try to tackle it first.

Federal, state, and local governments spend billions of tax dollars each year to correct social problems and alleviate deficiencies in the human condition—through the public schools! Newspaper columnists often blame schools for *creating* social problems. But drug abuse, sexual promiscuity, alcoholism, and vandalism all stem from the sins of our society. In one way or another, we parents have failed to deal with that sin at home and in our communities; so we must share the blame for the consequences.

Let's make a confession: We Christian parents have expected the public schools to deal with the symptoms of our problems, as everyone else does. We've wanted our schools to suppress any socially undesirable behavior. But we've gotten angry when our children were the objects of that suppression.

For example, we don't want a person to appear drunk in public; so we get upset when a high school student comes to school drunk. But what do we do about it? Do we expect the principal to reprimand the student and tell him to "go home and sober up"? Do we want the principal to call in the student's parents for a conference? Should the student be suspended for several days? What other disciplinary action might be taken? Most parents would say that school officials ought to do *something* to suppress this drunken behavior.

Yet I have to ask, "What caused the student's drinking problem? And how are we going to deal with the cause?" Start a high school chapter of Alcoholics Anonymous? Sounds like a simple solution. But again, we would be dealing with a symptom, not the *cause* of the student's problem.

Most conflicts between parents and school officials begin here. Parents and school officials have different ideas about what behavior they should encourage and what they should suppress. They disagree about the methods to be used to suppress undesirable behavior. So when Jimmy staggers in drunk and gets punished, Mom and Dad draw the battle lines.

Parents and school personnel should try to set common goals of acceptable behavior. My elderly friends say, "If I got a whipping at school, I knew that when I got home my dad was going to whip me twice as hard!" A child need not be disciplined that way in all situations. But the old "second whipping" method illustrated one thing—that the school and the home worked together. They did not pull a child in two different directions. They provided consistent training for the child's life. We need that kind of moral consistency today.

Why Have Public Schools?

Christian parents may ask, "Why have public schools anyway? What's the value of government-sponsored schools?"

Let me try to answer. I'll begin with my nutshell definition of the purpose of public education:

It is the purpose of public education to develop in all students the skills and attitudes that will enable them to deal positively with their environment, to develop all that is good for themselves and for others.

Read the definition again. If I've been able to describe the *purpose* of public education here, it should help us draw up a good *plan* for public education. So read it again and ask yourself, "Is this definition valid? Does this really describe what public education is all about?"

If you accept my definition, you'll begin to see a most interesting thing. You'll realize that our public schools should give youth the basic vocational and technical skills they need, of course. But you'll notice that our schools should also give them the ability to make sound decisions. Our schools should train young people to discriminate between what is good and bad, constructive and destructive, beneficial and harmful.

The Christian would go one step farther. He would say, *The schools should encourage our youth to interact with other people in ways that honor the Lord.* At the very least, a Christian parent says, "Our schools should not wreck the moral standards of Christian young people."

By now you have a good notion of how I would answer those three basic questions I raised earlier.

Yes, I believe our schools exert an important influence upon students' behavior.

I think our schools often exert a negative or detrimental influence.

And yet, I believe parents can help to reverse the trend. Surely we can do more than stand on the sidelines and jeer.

A Shift in Values

Never have the majority of people in this country lived by the Judeo-Christian ethic. There has never

14

been a "moral majority," despite many well-meaning people who argue to the contrary. However, at the turn of the century most people *acknowledged* the Judeo-Christian ethic. Just before World War I, American parents and children knew certain social behaviors were acceptable and others were unacceptable. School officials felt obliged to enforce this Judeo-Christian standard; they made sure that students behaved in the prescribed manner.

At that time, most communities would have been scandalized if their lady school teacher smoked. Of if she married. Perish the thought! (My aunt eloped and kept her marriage a secret, because her school board would have dismissed her from teaching.) And a school teacher who got a divorce might as well find another profession. Today we may feel some of these standards were not based on the Judeo-Christian ethic; but then people felt they were! And school officials tried to up-hold the standards.

The famous trial of John Scopes in Cleveland, Tennessee, showed how earnestly school officials tried to guard the religious standards of their constituents. It was the first time the teaching of evolution had ever been challenged in public court. Many biology teachers secretly supported John Scopes; but they knew he clashed with the convictions of people in their communities. They respected those convictions, even if they did not agree with them.

I suspect that teachers have always rubbed against some ideals of the communities they serve. But only in recent years has the public started thinking about this friction. A few crusading Christian leaders say the rift is so wide that they can never trust public school officials; they say all of them are "humanistic and anti-Christian." I know by firsthand experience that's not so. But the controversy grabs headlines.

The more we deplore our differences, the wider we make them. And the harder it is for our young people to cross the rift between their parents and teachers.

Abandoning Our Schools

We Christian parents have often abandoned the public schools. We have transferred our children to private schools. Or we've kept our children in the public schools and refused to get involved with what happens there. Here's how:

Usually, the elementary school is still a neighborhood school. Your children walk or ride a very short distance to their elementary school (unless you live in a large city with a massive school busing program or in a sparsely populated rural area). They know the other children who attend that school; you know the children's parents. They live in your neighborhood. You feel close to them.

Since the school is in your neighborhood, you feel close to the principal and teachers who work there, too. You are apt to visit the classroom now and then. You are likely to be involved in the P.T.A., since you know the parents *and* the teachers there. You are an active parent.

Then your child grows up and attends middle school, junior high, and high school. Now he travels a greater distance to school. He jostles through the hall with hundreds or thousands of other students every day—students who commute to the school from just as great a distance in the opposite direction. He doesn't know his classmates; you don't know their parents. It's more of a chore to visit the school or attend P.T.A. So you stop doing those things. You become a dropout parent.

But the parent and the teacher must work together to educate a young person. They should link the home and the school together. In his perceptive book, *How to Improve Your Child's Education*, John Dobbert says, "Parents have turned over much of their training responsibilities to adults outside the home, usually school personnel."⁴ He's right. And it has to change.

Christians often speak of training "up a child in the way he should go" (Proverbs 22:6); but too many parents do not understand what is meant by the word *train*. It means being actively involved in the education process.

I've *taught* my Labrador retriever not to go into my vegetable garden. But on a hot day Jack sneaks into the garden and lies down between the bean rows to get cool. If he hears me coming, he slinks out of the garden with his tail between his legs. I needn't tell him to leave; he knows he should. But if I want to *train* him, I'll have to spend more time with Jack (giving him punishments and rewards, and so on) until he changes that habit. Likewise many of us have instructed our children what is right and wrong to do. But we must spend time with our children if we expect to give them real training. We'll know they're trained—not just taught—when we see them change the way they act.

I don't think a parent should "check up" on a child regularly; that would be spying! But you ought to investigate when your child begins acting oddly. For example, when my oldest daughter was in the first grade, she began bringing home money that we had not given her. Not large amounts of money—ten cents or so every day. My wife and I were concerned about where she was getting the money. So we made inquiry at school concerning any missing money. Both the teacher and secretary said everything was fine.

Finally, I asked my daughter.

"Oh, that's my picture money," she replied.

"Picture money?"

"Yes. At recess I draw pictures of the big kids and sell them. They really like what I draw."

This cute little first grader had gone into business for herself! The older kids were giving her a nickel or a dime for her custom-made portraits. That episode made me feel a little silly because of the outcome. But it's not always so. If you notice unusual behavior in your child, start asking discreet questions about what is going on.

When you send your child to school, you invest a part of yourself in the school. It becomes your school. Don't talk disparagingly of "those people at the school," for in a very real sense *you* are at the school now. From the parents' point of view, it's so much easier not to be involved. We hope our schools will do a good job of training our children. And as long as the schools meet our expectations, we keep quiet. But if they don't, they will hear us loud and clear!

The most strident critics of our public schools are people who feel they have been ignored by the church, the schools, and other institutions of society. They fold their arms and silently defy those institutions; and they come out swinging their fists when they feel dissatisfied enough. They're not making the decisions and carrying the load of those institutions, so they lash out at the people who are. Christians do this as much as anyone else.

George Van Alstine has published a fascinating study of the history of public education in America. He says, "Thus far public schools have not shunned Christians as much as Christians have shunned public schools. The door for our involvement is wide open. Only our fear, our passivity, or our preoccupation with other interests keeps Christian parents from taking advantage of the opportunities to influence public education."[5]

Let's begin building bridges between the home and the school—bridges of understanding and cooperation. Parents and teachers could travel in both directions upon such a bridge. We can tell school teachers our ideas and aspirations for our children, and they can tell us theirs. Together we can forge a partnership to train our children—academically, morally, and spiritually—to become mature adults.

Granted, we will not always agree with our school officials. There are times when we must be a "stone of offense" to the world just as Christ was (1 Peter 2:7, 8). But notice how Christ was "offensive"—He stood for what was right, even when the world disagreed with Him. That's the only reason Christians should be offensive, the only reason we should disagree with others. For when we stand for what's right, we have every reason to hold our ground.

Shortly after the Falkland Islands crisis, a reporter said to Prime Minister Margaret Thatcher, "In America you're known as 'The Iron Lady.' I wonder how you feel about being called that?"

"Well, if your convictions are not worth standing up for, what is the use of having them?" Mrs. Thatcher replied.

The same is true of the Christian. At times the Christian will offend others with his convictions. He should never say, "I'm going to pick a fight with that guy so he'll know I'm a force to be reckoned with." But he must say, "I must tell these people how I feel, even if they disagree with me." Jesus said that we must be "wise as serpents" in dealing with the world (Matthew 10:16); but remember He also told us to be "harmless as doves" in our attitudes.

One other word of caution: Don't expect to make grand, sweeping changes in your school. Change is not apt to come in such a manner. It's more likely that large numbers of Christian parents will bring gradual, consistent change, punctuated by occasional spurts of visible progress. We like to have "instant" everything, but let's face it—some things do not happen instantly. The Lord may not allow us to see the fruit of our work right away.

Don't Wait for a Blowup

Christian parents too often get involved in school

after what I call "a significant emotional event"—in other words, a crisis. A teacher does something that provokes the parents. A principal ignores drug dealing in the halls. The school board decides to close the neighborhood school. This crisis draws a hostile reaction from John Christian; he reacts quickly and forcefully. He fears for his children; he doesn't want them harmed. So he plunges into the fray. And in the heat of the moment, he may act in a rather un-Christian fashion.

I once made a snide remark to one of my students that hurt her deeply. I got a phone call from her mother. She was hostile, and I was pretty hostile in return. After a ten-minute verbal barrage, she hung up on me. Neither of us were Christians at that time, and in the heat of the moment we vented some rather nasty emotions. We've both become Christians since them; the Lord has healed our relationship; and we are now close friends. We learned that we needed to work together, in good times and bad.

We have so many demands pressing in upon us. We must earn a paycheck, keep the house clean, and take care of all the other responsibilities of raising a family. So we would just as soon leave the schools alone, unless there's a crisis. Yet the moment of crisis is the worst possible time to start taking an interest in schools; there is too much tension and hostility to let us "get acquainted" with our school officials then.

Staying in Touch

Well, how can we stay in touch with our school officials?

We get information about our schools through the newspaper, radio, TV, or other media. But most of the information will come through our own children. What a child says about the teacher, the principal, and his classmates will shape our impression of the whole school environment. We may get a good deal of misinformation through our children. I'm not saying that they're untruthful. But we should take into account the special perspective each child has on the situation.

Let's say that one of your children is a little girl, a first grader. She will see her school much differently than her brother, who's a seventeen-year-old football player. And neither of them will see the school quite like you would if you were there, observing the situation through the eyes of an adult.

M. Dale Baughman is a popular speaker at educators' conferences. He's always able to see the humor in education. (And believe me, educators could use a good laugh now and then!) Mr. Baughman says, "My six-year-old, Dlynn Lea, was attending a P.T.A. meeting with us. Listening attentively to the words of the presiding official, she suddenly tensed and became obviously apprehensive. When I asked for an explanation, she reminded me that the speaker had said, 'Let's get a second to the motion, and then the floor will be thrown open.'"[6]

I wonder how that little girl might have reported the meeting to her dad if he had not been there!

The best way to stay in touch with what is happening at your school is to *be there* as often as you can. Interact with your school officials in meaningful ways.

Get acquainted with your child's teacher early in the year. (See the chapter on "The Teacher and the Principal" for some practical hints.)

Stop by the principal's office and introduce yourself.

Attend P.T.A. meetings regularly, and offer to serve in some capacity.

If you can arrange the time in your weekly schedule, volunteer to be a teacher's aide. (See the chapter on "Volunteers" for more details.)

If that kind of involvement is not feasible for you, offer to help with a school outing now and then. Take the class on a tour through your place of business.

There are literally dozens of ways you might stay in touch with your school. In the following chapters, I will suggest more of them. But why not use your own imagination right now to thing of some other ways you can get involved? How might you be true to your school? Jot down some ideas and try them. Your school officials will thank you. And someday your child will, too.

NOTES

[1]"Blast Your Critics with Education's Good News," *The American School Board Journal,* June 1980, pp. 20, 21.

[2]*Ibid.,* p. 22.

[3]*Ibid.,* p. 22.

[4]John Dobbert, *How to Improve Your Child's Education* (Irvine, CA: Harvest House Publishers, 1980), p. 188.

[5]George Van Alstine, *The Christian and the Public Schools* (Nashville, TN: Abingdon Press, 1982), pp. 95, 96.

[6]M. Dale Baughman, *The Educator's Handbook of Stories, Quotes, and Humor* (Englewood Cliffs, NJ: Prentice-Hall, 1963), no. 248.

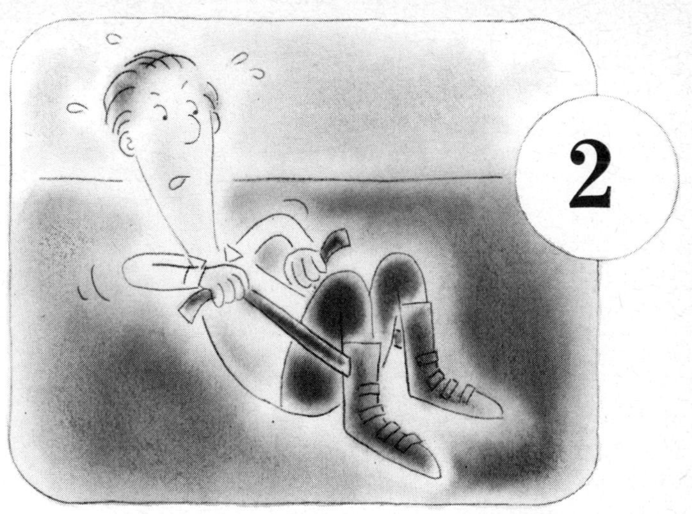

Humanism

While I was a graduate student at the University of Illinois, I learned that man could use his own reasoning power to create an ideal society, free from the repressive shackles of religion. That's the way many of my professors and classmates viewed religion—as something that restricts and hinders man from becoming all that he might be. In fact, many innovative thinkers of this century have this idea, which is commonly known as *humanism.*

The champions of humanism say that it is the best hope of mankind. They would like to have humanism ingrained in the thinking of our young people; and, of course, one way to do that is to emphasize humanism in our public schools.

Some Christian parents recognize this trend. They've read books by Francis A. Schaeffer, John Whitehead, and other Christian thinkers who warn that humanism is a menace in the public schools. However, most parents are bewildered by all the talk about humanism. They're not sure what humanism is, and they wonder whether or not it's a real threat to their children's values.

Two Faiths

The humanist has a faith, just as the Christian does. The humanist places his faith in the sovereignty of man's reason and the ultimate self-perfection of man. The evangelical Christian places his faith in the sovereignty of God's Word and the ultimate salvation of man. You may think this is just an abstract issue for theologians and philosophers to argue about, but humanism may dictate the approach your school officials will take toward your child. So we should take a moment to compare these two faiths.

Humanists don't believe that God reveals any truth to us. They believe that a person must find truth on his own terms—through the scientific method, philosophical reflection, experimental relationships, etc. But they reject the idea that God (or any human authority representing God) could reveal anything of real value in their quest for the meaning of life.

On the other hand, we Christians believe that God revealed His love for us through Jesus Christ and through the written Word of Scripture. We believe that the Bible

    ... describes the ultimate destiny of man,

    ... prescribes the only solution for his guilt and lostness, and

    ... provides a reliable guide for daily living.

All other conflicts between humanists and Christians stem from this basic conflict about the source of truth.[1] While the humanist searches for truth through his personal experience of philosophical theory, the Christian expects God to reveal the truth he needs through Scripture.

The humanist can't satisfy his hunger for truth. Every time he seeks the meaning of life in some new experience or ideology, he finds void and emptiness. So he tries a more offbeat experience of a more unorthodox ideology, and he finds that his life is just as empty and meaningless as before. The humanist believes his hunger is insatiable because he keeps having new needs to be met. But the Christian believes it is because the humanist seeks truth (in this case the meaning of life) in the wrong place.

I've learned that most humanists lack personal or corporate identity. They crave attention that will give them a label of some sort. In July, 1969, our country was waist-deep in Vietnam, teenagers were joining the drug scene, and many students rebelled against authority. I was enrolled in a graduate psychology class. The professor assembled a panel of seven hippie-looking guys, who sat on the platform to be questioned by our class. These seven guys were not kids; they were all in their late twenties. They had long hair. They wore beads, headbands, sandals (or were barefoot), and had lots of tattoos. Definitely not the type I'd want my daughter to marry! Someone in the audience asked, "Don't the police get suspicious of you just because of the way you look?"

One of the older members of the group said, "Sure, man. The cops hassle us all the time."

Someone else then asked, "Which is worse—to be hassled by the cops or be ignored totally."

After a brief pause, the leader said, "I'd rather be hassled, man. Why do you think I look like this, anyway?"

Nineteenth-century humanists such as Henry David Thoreau and Ralph Waldo Emerson said that man is basically good. They believed society has made man evil so he must be liberated from the restraints of society.[2] Modern humanists echo this theme. They also believe that the stodgy guardians of tradition use

Christianity to repress human individuality and uniqueness. They believe Christianity is just a tool used to squelch human freedom.

But we Christians disagree. We believe that a person can realize his unique potential only by living in Jesus Christ. We say that only by being surrendered to Christ can a person develop and utilize the abilities he has. Genesis 1:26 says, "And God said, Let us make man in our image, after our likeness: and let them have dominion." Only man was created in God's own image. Only man was afforded the privilege of having dominion over all the rest of creation. Only man has personal fellowship with God. Only man has an immortal soul. And only man can become a "child of God" by accepting Jesus Christ as his Savior (John 1:12). Who can say this is a demeaning view of man? We don't believe it is. We contend that the gospel of Jesus Christ is ennobling and liberating in every way.

The Moral Impact of Humanism

You may be thinking, "So what? This still sounds like philosophical gobbledygook. What does humanism have to do with me? How does it affect the way my children are taught at school?"

The greatest impact of humanism is in the area of morals. The humanist does not believe that God presides over the universe; even the theistic humanist (a humanist who believes in God) would say that God stands aloof from the everyday affairs of man. Humanists believe that man has control of the world; he's free to do whatever he feels is most beneficial to himself. This approach is called *pragmatism*. Imagine how a humanist might use pragmatism.

A pragmatist tries to achieve the simplest and most direct solutions to her moral problems. Her unwanted baby is aborted before birth. Or if she chooses to let the baby be born, and the child has a birth defect, she allows the infant to die without corrective surgery. The pragmatist tells her doctor to "take care of" her mother who has terminal cancer by withholding further treatment. As you can see, the pragmatist's way of handling moral problems can be brutal; and a pragmatic humanist can perpetrate gross inhumanity in the name of "humanism."

The evangelist Leighton Ford was talking with a humanistic college student. The student said he did not understand how God could have allowed Adolf Hitler to kill six million Jews. Surely there was no God, was there?

Reflecting on that question later, Mr. Ford said, "If there is no God, what's *wrong* with killing six million Jews?" If there are no moral standards of what is right, except 'what is good for society,' what's to keep a Hitler from determining what is good for society? This is a serious chink in the logic of humanism.

Consider what is happening right now in the United States. Each year over 1.2 million abortions are performed; we destroy enough babies to repopulate the city of Detroit. That's revolting to the Christian. But the humanist thinks this is a very pragmatic way to dispose of unwanted pregnancies. If an abortion relieves the trauma a young mother is experiencing, the humanist says, "Go ahead and do it." But how will she feel in the future? What about her guilt and trauma *after* the abortion? What about the moral consequences of destroying a human life now? What happens to a society that permits physicians to *destroy* healthy human lives, for a fee?

First Corinthians 3:11 says, "Other foundation can no man lay than that is laid, which is Jesus Christ." The chilling moral consequences of humanism prove it. When man builds his moral foundations upon the shifting sands of "what's best for me," or "what's best for society," rather than building upon Christ, he soon finds that he's living in a macabre "House of Usher."

Humanism and Your Teacher

In 1933 the American Humanist Association drafted a document called "The Humanist Manifesto." They revised the Manifesto and published it again in 1973. One of their goals, according to the Manifesto, is *to control public education at all levels.* And the American Humanist Associate has made considerable progress toward that goal. Other organizations such as the National Organization for Women (NOW), the Sex Information and Education Council of the United States (SIECUS), and Planned Parenthood want to influence the public schools with their humanistic ideals. They are convincing our educators with seminars, films, and tons of free literature. And some educators have bought their line. They have adopted a humanistic outlook on life.

So how does humanism affect what our educators do? How does it affect their teaching?

Remember that humanism says each person should have opportunity to reach his fullest potential. Therefore, humanistic teachers should care more about their students than teachers ever have before. Often this is true. Humanistic teachers are very caring individuals. Both the humanistic teacher and the Christian teacher want the pupil to reach his full potential.

But the humanistic teacher feels he can best reach that goal through scientific inquiry, philosophical dialogue, and values clarification. The Christian teacher feels the student can best fulfill his potential by surrendering his life to Jesus Christ, by coming to know the truth of God's Word, and by accepting the moral principles that are in God's Word.

Neither of these approaches is stated explicitly in the classroom. But it's in the back of the teacher's mind. It forms the standard by which the teacher gauges the student's progress toward real fulfillment and stability in life.

So far we've been looking at the vehicle that the teacher uses for training a child. We should also consider the destination. What sort of person does the humanistic teacher want her pupil to be? "The Humanist Manifesto" says a person who is truly "liberated" and "self-actuated" will not depend upon God. He will evaluate each moral decision in pragmatic terms ("What's best for myself or my society?"). These ideals are in strong conflict with the ideals a Christian teacher would have for her students.

Take the case of two imaginary teachers, "Linda Liberated" and "Bernie Bible." Linda is a humanist, and Bernie is an evangelical Christian (in case you hadn't guessed). Linda teaches a twelfth-grade course in modern American history; Bernie teaches the same course across the hall. Both of them are intelligent, well-educated people. Both have a master's degree from a nearby state university. Both follow the *syllabus* (teaching plan) that the State Board of Education drew up for the course. Same textbooks. Same test questions. Everything Linda and Bernie do is the same.

Or is it?

You see, their purpose is not the same. Linda wants her students to set their own moral standards, even if they fly against the standards of their parents and everyone else. Bernie wants his students to have God-honoring moral standards, and to respect the standards of everyone else. He wants them to develop their talents and skills without taking advantage of other people. Now let's see how Linda and Bernie lead a typical class session.

Today they're giving an oral exam on the Vietnam War. Remember, their students have had the same textbooks. And now Linda and Bernie will ask identical questions from the prescribed teaching plan. Listen to what they say.

Linda asks, "Why did the *United States* get involved in the Vietnam conflict?" (Her tone of voice implies,

"What business did we have there, anyway? Why didn't we stay home?")

Bernie asks, "Why *did* the United States get involved in the Vietnam conflict?" (He implies, "Our involvement was a fact. Apparently our leaders thought we should get involved. What reasons did they have?")

Next question. Linda says, "If you had been drafted to fight in Vietnam, would you have gone? Why or *why not?*" (Implied, "I would not expect you to have gone. So tell me why.")

Bernie says, "If you had been drafted to fight in Vietnam, would you have gone? *Why* or why not?" (Implied, "I would expect you to go. I would expect you to obey the law, even if you disagree with the lawmakers. Tell me why you would.")

This may seem like a very subtle sort of manipulation. It is! But Linda and Bernie could influence their students more overtly. Suppose a student said, "Now that you've heard our opinion, Miss Liberated/Mr. Bible, what do *you* think? What would *you* have done?" Not one school board in America could stop these teachers from answering. And do you suppose Linda and Bernie will answer that question in the same way? Of course not. Their moral standards are different, and they want their students' moral standards to be different.

How to Counteract Humanism

We Christians need not withdraw from the problems of our world; but we should learn how to lovingly invade the world. This is certainly true in our dealings with humanism.

If a group of outraged Christian parents enter their school and try to remove everything from the curriculum that they believe is humanistic, how many well-meaning teachers will they trample in the process? When we're tempted to yank the "tares" out of our schools, let's be sure we're not destroying good "wheat" at the same time. A vindictive crusade can hurt students and educators just as much as the humanism itself. If we approach the problem with rabid hostility, we will teach everyone a tragic lesson about Christianity—a tragically wrong lesson.

Paul Stookey earned stardom as part of the group "Peter, Paul, and Mary." He toured hundreds of college campuses in the late 1960s and 1970s. He's still touring, in fact (as a gospel singer now), because Paul has given his life to the Lord Jesus Christ. I heard him sing at the Praise Gathering for Believers (an annual Christian rally held at the Indianapolis Convention Center) in November of 1982. Paul sang several gospel songs. Then he sang "Puff the Magic Dragon." He had to explain the message of the song, though. He told us a lot of Christians didn't like this song when they first recorded it. They said the group was trying to promote marijuana or some other kind of drug. But they had nothing like that in mind. It was just a fantasy song for children, and the group liked it.

Christians get so angry about certain things. Some always "see red." He didn't realize that till he became a Christian himself.

He's right, you know.

Humanism is a serious problem in our schools. But let's not get so angry about humanism that we "see red" in everything our schoolteachers do. Let's be calm. And if humanism *is* being taught in our schools, let's deal with it in a firm but loving way.

Humanism in the schools is not easy to identify or to fix. We can't just set a time, car pool to the neighborhood school, and administer our "quick fix" to humanism. Humanism has moved into our schools quite gradually, and it must be removed gradually. The remedy will require a long-term commitment to our public schools, and a crystal-clear recognition of the problem. Excellent Christian books are being published on this subject—the best-known being Tim LaHaye's *The Battle for the Mind.* [3]*We should delve into these books to learn all that we can about the challenge that confronts us. We must also realize that not all the problems discussed in such a book are present in all schools.*

We can counteract humanism by supporting our Christian politicians. Christians should enter the political process at every level, supporting candidates who uphold moral standards of Scripture (even if they are not Christians themselves). And certainly more Christian parents should run for political office.

I think I know why so few Christians run for political office. It's because we're afraid of defeat. We may be defeated the first time we run for office. But each time we run, we are more likely to be elected because more people are acquainted with our names. Humanists seem to understand this process better than Christians do; and they are persistent.

Also, we should make sure the news media understands our views. For example, we should write letters to the editor of our local newspapers (and sign our names!). Christians in this country have too often adopted a pietist view that says, "We shouldn't involve ourselves in the affairs of the world—we might get our hands dirty." But we *must* get involved if the shapers of public policy are ever going to know what we Christians care about.

Finally, we should be prepared to be verbally attacked! Humanists are quite ready to call us narrow, right-wing fundamentalists who are trying to destroy their constitutional freedoms. *We should not try to respond to our critics;* we should simply speak the truth. If we try to defend our integrity, we lend credibility to their accusations.

I hesitated to write this chapter. Christian writers have often portrayed the public school system as a den of humanism, corrupted beyond all hope. Obviously, I disagree. It's true that humanism is influencing our educators; but most educators have allowed this unwittingly. I believe that when we make them aware of the strong conflict between humanism and traditional Judeo-Christian ideals, many of them will begin making changes.

Humanists certainly have a right to believe what they believe; that is the genius of American democracy. But Christians have just as much a right to say, "Christianity is a valid, honorable way of life. We expect our public schools to honor our Christian standards as well as the humanists' standards ... for the sake of our children's future."

NOTES

[1]Christians often assume that their basic conflict with humanists is about the existence of God; but many humanists believe that God exists. They have a man-oriented view of God's moral standards; they believe that God did not inspire the writing of Scripture. Yet they do believe that God exists. Theologians call these humanists *theists* (God-believers). They believe in the existence of a Supreme Being, but they reject virtually everything else of the Christian faith. But most humanists are *atheists* (believe there is no God) or *agnostics* (believe we cannot know anything about God if He does exist).

[2]Karl Marx also believed this. He argued that there is something inherently evil in a capitalistic society's hierarchy of power which tends to corrupt man. So Marx's ultimate goal was to destroy the hierarchy. Let the masses be the ruling authority, he reasoned. Let them determine moral rightness and wrongness.

[3]Tim LaHaye, *The Battle for the Mind* (Old Tappan, NJ: Fleming H. Revell, 1980).

The Teacher and the Principal

As a parent, you are the most influential person in your child's life. Who's the next most influential? It might be his schoolteacher. (During your child's earlier years, you may get the message, from your child, that you don't know much and the teacher knows it all.) That's why you should get to know your child's teacher, and do all that you can to establish a positive relationship.

Teachers are under a tremendous amount of pressure these days. Government budgets are tight, so teachers have fewer resources for doing their job. Classes are being enlarged. Some teachers' jobs are being eliminated. Place these things alongside the growing demand for academic excellence in our public schools, and you begin to understand why your teacher needs some encouragement!

Schoolteachers often say they are treated like little more than high-priced baby-sitters. (Or worse, *unwanted* baby-sitters.) They get that notion from the indifferent attitude that many parents have toward them. Many parents never visit the classroom ... never attend an open house ... aren't interested in P.T.A....and skip parent-teacher conferences. They act as though the school is just a place to park their kids for a few hours each day. Is it any wonder the teachers feel like baby-sitters?

Another source of pressure is unionism. Teachers' unions may cause division between school boards and teachers—also between striking and nonstriking teachers. Some of my friends who chose not to strike when their teachers' union went out on the picket lines have suffered some pretty grim harassment. Few teachers will use the violent tactics that a union may want to employ. But some do. Windows are smashed. Tires are slashed. Bomb threats are phoned to the schools. That's when unions create a rift *between teachers* in the same school. (Fortunately, that is not always the case and local teacher groups are sometimes able to work positively in cooperation with school officials for the benefit of all.)

Given all of these pressures, I think most of our teachers are doing an excellent job. Have you made an effort to reach out to your teacher to show your support? You probably will find that the teacher is ready to work with you. School officials care about you and your child, more than you might realize; they will demonstrate this to an even greater degree when you show that you are an interested, supportive parent.

Some principals require their teachers to make one positive contact with a parent every day. The teacher might go into the office, make a phone call to a parent, and say, "I just wanted you to know what a super job Johnny did leading the pledge of allegiance this morning. He wasn't as nervous this time."

Qualities of a Good Teacher

Cliff Schimmels has compiled an interesting list of the "Qualities of a Good Teacher."[1] Let me share that list of qualities, and make a few comments on each one:

1. *"Good teachers read and hand back homework assignments."* If homework is important enough to be done, it's important enough to be read by the teacher. Students should have some assurance that their teacher is reading and evaluating those stacks of papers they turn in. The new elementary school reading programs often require a great deal of paperwork.

2. *"Good teachers give worthwhile assignments."* Time is valuable; teachers shouldn't waste children's time on busy work. Schimmels recalls that when one high school teacher asked a student to stay after school to finish work on a project, the student said, "No, I have too much homework to do. I have to copy 96 sentences for placement of commas." That teacher was lazy. If she wanted to train students in placing commas, why didn't she have the sentences mimeographed?

3. *"Good teachers stay in the classroom,"* Schimmels says. "The best way to check this is to listen to your child's stories. If he has too many tales of eraser fights and classroom chaos, the teacher is probably having coffee problems." If that really is true, talk to your principal. In most schools, the principal can change coffee-break privileges if teachers are abusing them. Every teacher will need to leave the classroom for a few minutes occasionally. But if it's a few minutes every hour, every day, then the teacher has a serious problem.

4. *"Good teachers decorate their rooms."* Bulletin boards, newspaper clippings, the students' own work, whatever the situation demands. Not all teachers are adept at this. I was a poor bulletin-board designer; but,

since I taught in high school, I could enlist the talent of some students who *were* good. Most elementary school-teachers can buy bulletin-board kits from their supply catalogs, kits with attractive and colorful designs for every season of the year.

When I was a junior high student, I had a history teacher named Richard Rothgeb who gave me a great deal of incentive to become a teacher. Many teenagers hate social studies and history, but Mr. Rothgeb made history come alive for us. One way he did this was with his bulletin board. It was located just to the left of the door as we entered the classroom. I can remember walking into that room and seeing three or four students gathered around the bulletin board every Monday morning to read what he had put there. If we were studying World War II, for example, he would put some original newspaper clippings on the board. Always he had something to pique our curiosity and motivate us to learn.

5. *"Good teachers are organized."* Good teachers know where they are going. Good students in their classes know where they are going." A child should know what the teacher expects of him. He should have a clear idea of the goals of the class session, what he is supposed to grasp by the time a particular study has ended. Some teachers don't convey this goal because they are too haphazard in their own preparation.

I'm not saying that a teacher must be perfectly organized. I have known some outstanding teachers who always had stacks of books and papers strewn across their desks. And, by the same token, I have known some poor teachers who had very neat desks and classrooms. But, generally speaking, a teacher who is well-organized and orderly will accomplish much more than one who is not.

6. *"Good teachers communicate with parents."* Teachers should ask for the parents' support. Some parents out there in the community wish they could get

involved in the schools, while teachers in the school wish the parents would get involved ... and one never approaches the other!

It's like two teenagers sitting in class, wishing they knew how to "break the ice" and get acquainted: The girl wishes the guy would ask her for a date, and the guy wishes he had the nerve to ask. But he doesn't ask. So they sit there and keep on wishing.

A good teacher makes sure that doesn't happen in the parent-teacher relationship. That teacher takes the initiative. She "breaks the ice" with a note, a phone call, or a visit and starts communication with the parent.

7. *"Good teachers don't lose control of themselves."* Schimmels adds that "teaching is a disease that attacks the nervous system first. . . .Teachers cannot respond to misbehavior with anger, maliciousness, or violence." We expect that a child might lose control of his emotions at times; but a teacher should never lose control. He may need to be firm with discipline. He may need to raise his voice now and then. But he must maintain full control of himself.

8. *"Good teachers don't lose control of the classroom."* Every class requires its own kind of control, of course. When I was directing a high school choir, I had to maintain fairly rigid control of what the students were doing. We had eighty-five singers in one of the choirs. Every one of them had to do the same thing at the same time in the same way in order to perform a song.

Not so in the art class meeting next door. There some students might be working with pottery kilns, others might be running a potter's wheel, others might be painting with oils, others might be carving wood, welding metal, or doing any number of other things. The art teacher had to give those students the freedom to work on independent projects. So the room was filled with noise—busy, purposeful noise.

If you had gone to the library and found a teacher

leading a class in a research project, you would have thought, "My, this seems like a lot of noise for a library!" But if you had stood and watched what was happening, you would have seen groups of two or three students huddled over various books discussing their work. You would have noticed they were busy and intensely interested in what they were learning. That was purposeful noise, too.

Then there's the classroom where the teacher turns her back, a spitball sails across the aisle, and everyone laughs!

One kind of noise is purposeful; the other is not. One kind of noise indicates control; the other does not. A good teacher maintains control of the class and guides it toward meaningful goals.

9. *"Good teachers give students a sense that the material is important."* In other words, they get the impression that this lesson will truly have an impact on their lives. If the lesson is not that important, why teach it?

Students will not always appreciate the importance of a lesson. For example, as I said before, most students do not like social studies—history, government, economics, and the like. Why? Because these subjects involve a great deal of reading? Perhaps. I can think of another reason though. Frankly, I believe our social studies teachers have done a poor job of "selling" their students on why it is important to study these subjects. If the students don't understand how they will profit by studying American government, world geography, climate, good production, and allied subjects related to them, they won't be interested!

If the teacher thinks the subject is really important, chances are that the students will think it's important. If the teacher feels a sense of urgency about the material being discussed, so will the students.

My daughter "turned on" to Indiana history in the fourth grade because her fourth-grade teacher was "turned on" by it. State law requires that Indiana history be taught in the fourth grade, and I'm sure many teachers do it in a perfunctory way. But this particular teacher loved Indiana history. She had visited many historical sites in the state with her camera, and she used her color slides to illustrate the lessons. When you walked into her room and saw the beautiful displays, you got the impression that Indiana history was the most important thing those students would learn in their twelve years of schooling! The students got that message.

10. *"Good teachers don't abuse their right to academic freedom."* For example, a teacher does not have the right to offend beliefs of a Jewish child, a Muslim child, or an atheistic child. The teacher has an obligation to love her students, not to convert them.

A few years ago, two educators published a book entitled, *Teaching as a Subversive Activity.*[2] They said that teachers have the right (even the *duty)* to try to win students over to their ideas. Why? Because teachers should be the vanguards of social change. They should plant progressive ideas and attitudes in the minds of their students. I disagree with that. I believe teachers should respect and perpetuate the existing values of our society—not revise them. Granted, every teacher will have personal views, and those views may deviate from what the public accepts. But "academic freedom" is not a license for a teacher to use the classroom to indoctrinate students in the teacher's personal views "for their own good."

If You Have Complaints . . .

What should you do if you suspect that your child has a poor teacher? Well, you certainly should not "cry wolf." If you complain about every little fault of every teacher, school officials will soon learn to ignore you. A hundred parents complaining once and independently are more likely to be heard than one parent who complains a hundred times. Some parents are notorious nitpickers. They come to the school two or three times each week to gripe about things that do not have much significance. "You moved my child's seat," or things of that sort. Eventually, the teacher and principal begin to think, "Oh, here comes Mrs. Terror again." They stop paying attention to the complaints.

So if you *do* have a complaint, give your school officials a little consideration. Make sure the issue is significant, something that will affect the life of your child or others.

Get the facts straight before you complain. I'm sure your child would never lie about a teacher (Would he?), but younger children may find it hard to distinguish between facts and their own imagination. Older children may tend to tell an incomplete version of what's happening. (Only the part they want you to hear!) So be sure you have the full story before you lodge a complaint.

Remember that the teacher is human. She may seem irritable for a period of time if her mother is in the hospital, if there are problems at home, or if she doesn't feel well. Other extenuating circumstances may cause her to do or say things that would not be normal. So talk with the teacher and find out her point of view before you start judging it. She's entitled to as much personal consideration as any other human being.

I've noticed that teachers seldom let their personal problems affect their work. In fact, they seem able to endure unusually tough circumstances without letting other people know. Two years ago a teacher in our school district discovered a mass in her side just two months before the end of the school term. The principal said to her, "You have accumulated plenty of sick leave. We can give someone else a temporary contract to finish the year. Why don't you take your leave and have surgery?" But she wouldn't hear of it; she intended to finish her assignment of teaching those children. After the term, she had the surgery and recovered nicely. I think you will find that most teachers, like her, handle stress unusually well. But teachers are human, too, and sometimes they make poor decisions or act in a less-than-ideal manner because of stress.

If you have a complaint about something the teacher has done, talk with the teacher first. If the problem can't be resolved that way, you can begin "going to the top"—through the building principal, the superintendent of schools, and the school board. Only if the problem is extremely serious should you consider going to civil court.

Remember that there are many individual differences among teachers. A few years ago, I took a couple of new school board members on a one-day tour of our school, so they could get acquainted with the teachers. Two classes next to each other gave us a clear-cut example of differences in teachers and teaching styles.

In one room, about three-fourths of the students were at their seats reading. The rest were in one corner of the room with the teacher. She had a book open on her lap while a couple of students sat beside her on chairs, a couple more were sitting Indian style on the floor, and one was lying on his belly—all of them intently involved in their reading group.

Then we walked to the next room. These students were of the same grade level, the same age level, and the same competency level. But here the teacher had all of the students seated except for six. They were lined up at the front of the room for a reading drill. It was a more authoritarian type of class environment, compared to the first room we'd visited. Yet the test scores of both classes showed that the teachers were equally successful in working with their students. The students in both rooms were learning the material and maturing in other ways, although the teachers' approaches were dramatically different.

What *can* you do about a really poor teacher?

Remember that we live in an era of unionism, and this affects public education as well as any other field. Just because a principal believes that someone is a poor teacher, he can't say, "We'll let him go next year." Union contracts and civil law prevent this sort of thing. A teacher who has served in a particular school for so many years has acquired *tenure,* and it's very difficult to dismiss a tenured teacher. You must prove the person is a poor teacher with exact times, places, and details of incidents. Very often the teacher will lodge a lawsuit to keep his job. And principals want to avoid a court trial if they possibly can.

Yet a principal can rid the school of a poor teacher. He may be able to do it more easily with your help, because you and others like you are the best source of documentation in such a case.

I know of a particular incident in which the teacher had, among other problems, a gruff personality that frightened the youngsters he was teaching. One parent even told the principal, "I have to spank my child to make him come to school sometimes, because he knows he'll be with Mr. X that day."

Each time a parent complained, the principal said, "Thank you for sharing this. We'll make a note of it in the teacher's file and talk with him about it." The principal could certainly not confide in those parents and say, "Thanks for this information. We are going to fire him as soon as we get enough material." I'm sure that frustrated many of the parents; but when the complaints kept coming in, they established a pattern that warranted dismissing the teacher. This particular teacher was also regarded by other teachers as a "displaced person." In other words, he was considered a poor teacher. He was warned about the problem. He had plenty of time to correct the problem, but he didn't. So his contract was not renewed—even though he had tenure.

At what point should you take a school problem to the news media. When should you write a letter to the editor or call the local TV station with a hot tip?

These methods seem far easier than trying to work through administrative channels. Some parents would rather draft a fiery letter to the editor and make the issue a community crusade, so that other parents will rally around to fight the battle for them. They don't have to invest the necessary time and effort needed to work the problem out. But "trial by newspaper" is not as easy as it may seem.

If the problem affects only *your* child—if you want the school to resolve a personal problem of some sort— it's not wise to focus community attention on your child.

In his book, *My Life Without God,* Bill Murray tells how agonizing the publicity was when his mother (then Madalyn Murray) sued his school for having prayer each day. His mother relished the fight. It gave her a chance to put atheism in the spotlight. But it also put young Bill in the spotlight, and his friends ridiculed him for it.

If your school has a serious problem that affects all of the students . . .

if you have prayed about the situation, and . . .

if you've concluded that the problem must be addressed publicly for the sake of the whole community . . .

then you might take the matter to the press. But be aware of the attendant dangers.

What Teachers Expect

I have shared a long list of things you should expect of a good teachers. But what should the teacher expect of you? Here are some things:

1. *Good parents are cooperative.* In other words, help the teacher educate your child. Suppose the teacher

says, "Susie is having some problems with her multi-plication tables. Since I have thirty-three children in my class this year, I'm not able to spend extra time with her. Could you work with her for the next two or three weeks, using these flash cards to help her learn?" Say yes. In fact, comply with any reasonable request that a teacher might make to help in the education of your child. These requests usually will be something you can easily do.

2. *Good parents are open and honest.* If there's some problem in the home that might cause your child to have temporary difficulties in school, let the teacher know. One family, who had a grandfather dying in a hospital a hundred miles away made the trip to see him twice a week—taking the children with them. The children were tired when they came to school the next day. The mother called their teacher and said, "Dad is on his deathbed, and we feel obliged to visit him. But this is going to make life rough for the kids the next few weeks. They won't be as alert as they normally should be. What can we do to help them?"

Teachers step into some awkward situations when parents fail to keep them informed. Several years ago, the band instructor came to my room one Monday afternoon with an ashen look on his face. At the beginning of band practice, he'd asked why one of the flute players was absent. This seventh-grade girl had been at school the previous Friday, but now she was gone with no explanation. He said, "Does anyone know what's the matter with _______?"

"Oh," one student replied, "she died last weekend."

At first the instructor thought it was a cruel joke. Something in that student's tone of voice kept him from laughing. Then he learned that the girl's appendix had burst Saturday night. Peritonitis had set in. And she had indeed died. But this was the first he'd heard of it.

3. *Good parents do not make unrealistic demands.*

This should go without saying. Yet some parents try to pressure a teacher into giving special favors to their children.

4. *Good parents go directly to the teacher when there is a problem.* This is simple courtesy. If someone had a complaint about the way you do your job at the office or factory, you would not want them to take it up with your supervisor. You'd want them to talk with you about it first. Remember Jesus' instructions for dealing with disputes in the community of faith (Matthew 18:15-17)? Your teacher deserves that much consideration, too.

5. *Good parents do not criticize the teacher in front of their child.* This open criticism gives the child a cynical view of the teacher and the whole school environment, which blunts his willingness to learn. As our friend M. Dale Baughman says, "Only a few teachers can keep the pot boiling when the fire is removed."[3] So don't let your criticism of the teacher douse *your* child's fire.

6. *Good parents do not believe everything their child says about the teacher.* 'Nuff said.

7. *Good parents make the teacher welcome in their home.* She can't make house calls to every home, as the old-fashioned country doctor did. But why not invite your teacher over for dinner sometime? You'll seldom be refused. The teacher will get to know you as friends, reinforcing the fact that you are *partners* in the work of educating your child.

Building Bridges! (or Mending Fences!)

How can you start your relationship with the teacher on the right foot? Or, if you've already known the teacher for awhile, how can you improve that relationship? Let me share a few ideas that may help:

If you go to school to pay fees a day or two before the sessions starts, you'll probably find the teacher getting the classroom ready. This is a good time for you to stop in for a brief get-acquainted visit. Keep it short. (If you stay too long—more than five minutes or so—you keep the teacher from getting the work done.) As you chat together, offer to help with her field trips, birthday parties, and other special occasions. Elementary teachers especially need to know this. My wife has often been asked to chaperon elementary field trips. Several parents go along on these trips, with a squad of students assigned to each one. (My wife is a good disciplinarian, so you can guess which students are usually assigned to her—the "active" ones!)

Send a note ahead of time if you know your child will be absent from school. The teacher will appreciate the advance notice, of course. But for the rest of the day she will feel good because of the P.S. you wrote at the bottom, which said, "Thank you for the good progress Joe is making in math." Or, "Sally really likes your class." Or, "I am grateful for the special attention you are giving Chris." Say something good about the teacher. Don't fabricate something—tell the truth! Remember that your teacher enjoys being praised for what she is doing.

If the teacher sends a note home for you to sign and return, add a personal note at the bottom. When my son Curtis was in the second grade, he was supposed to copy a note from the chalkboard every Friday and bring it home for us to sign and return. It was a kind of handwriting practice. The note might say, "This week we are learning about subtraction," or something similar. But it gave us a good opportunity to send the teacher a note in return.

If you are a Christian, you might send the teacher a note that says, "I pray for you every day." I don't think any teacher would be offended by that. Most of the teachers I know admit they need all the help they can get. Or you could offer some other word of encouragement. Here are some other things you can do:

1. *Attend the school's open house.* Sometime in the

month of October or November, most public schools will have an "open house" to coincide with National Education Week. Elementary schools may actually call it an "open house." Middle schools or junior highs may have a "swap day" (when students stay home and parents attend class in their place).

High schools may not plan any special activity because the parents have failed to show an interest. If that's true at your high school, talk with the principal and/or the P.T.A. president about beginning an annual open house there. Many parents feel uncomfortable about visiting their high school. They may know the head basketball coach, the drama coach, and the choir director; but the rest of the teachers are strangers to them. That's unfortunate. If you don't have a formal occasion to meet the teachers, create such an occasion, because you ought to know who is teaching your son or daughter in high school.

Granted, an "open house" or "swap day" will not show you a typical day at your school. But it will give you an opportunity to meet your teachers and school officials—an opportunity you might not take otherwise.

2. *Make an appointment with the teacher to discuss your child's progress.* This is especially important if you detect your child is having some problem academically, socially, or otherwise. (The open house is not a good time to discuss such problems. Other parents will be standing around and need to see the teacher, too.)

Most teachers will be happy to arrange a conference with you. (If yours is not, mention this to your principal.)

When the appointed hour arrives, greet the teacher with a smile. Thank her for the good job she has been doing with Susie or Johnny. Then calmly explain the reason for your concern. *Don't* suggest that the teacher is incompetent or unethical. But explain that you need her help in this situation, because she is an important person in the life of your child. Reassure the teacher that Susie really likes her class.

This conference should cause the teacher to make a real effort to solve your child's problem. Most teachers want to help your child, even if it requires extra effort to do so. Most teachers do not want to offend your moral standards or religious beliefs, and they will take steps to avoid offending you, even if they disagree strongly with you.

3. *Pray for the teacher.* You want your child to be successful in school. So does the teacher. You may disagree about the criteria for success; but you do agree that you want the best for your child. Pray that God will guide the teacher in training your child. Pray that the school environment will be conducive to learning and good character development. Pray that your child will respond well to the training he or she receives. I'm sure God will honor your prayers, for He wants your child to succeed, too!

The Principal

The single most important person in setting the tone of your school—the academic tone, the social tone, and the spiritual tone—is your principal. While the principal can guide the school's written curriculum to some extent, his greatest impact is upon the unwritten curriculum. He or she shapes the environment in which learning takes place. A school is but the shadow of the principal; his or her personality holds the corporate personality of the school.

A few years ago, I visited the principal of a large elementary school in a nearby city. It was about to begin a federally-mandated busing program to achieve racial integration. This particuliar school was predominantly black, but the principal was a white man. As we talked, I could see that he had a great deal of compassion for the parents of his pupils. That morning he had helped a woman who was trying to raise her children alone. "Her furnace goes out sometimes," he said, "so she calls me. She lives only three blocks away, and I go over there and relight the furnace for her. But next year her children will be bused to the other side of town; nobody will come from that school and relight her furnace. You can be sure of that!"

That principal set the tone of parent-teacher relations, didn't he?

A principal sets the tone of relationships inside the school, too. The relations between teacher and student.

For example, if the principal believes strict discipline is important, most of the teachers will use strict discipline. A few of the teachers may not like the pattern, so they will tend to drift out of the school over the course of several years. The principal may ease them out the door (overtly or otherwise) and replace them with teachers who will handle student discipline as he expects.

If the principal uses profane language, then some members of the staff will probably use profanity and, likewise, some of the students. But if the principal objects to profanity, smoking, and drinking, the staff is less likely to indulge in them. Neither will the students (at least not openly).

Parents often have the notion that Christians can do nothing in the public schools—no Bible reading, no prayer, etc. But there are great differences in the public schools of our country. Liberals have banded together to make a strong and aggressive power group in some areas of the country; there you'll find it difficult to have any Christian activities in the school. Yet other schools have Christian organizations such as the "Fellowship of Christian Athletes" or "Youth for Christ" operating openly and freely. What accounts for the difference? The parents and the open expectations of the local community. But the principal also is a factor. He or she decides how the school will respond to the parents' expectations. The principal might be called the gatekeeper of change. He or she often decides whether Christian clubs can meet in the school — or whether any other Christian activities can go on.[4] At other times the power may be in the hands of the superintendent, the school board, or a court.

The principal usually decides who is hired to teach. In many school corporations, the principal interviews each prospective teacher. Though the superintendent signs the teacher's contract, he consults with the principal before the choice is made.

Get acquainted with your principal early in the school year. In fact, you might stop by the principal's office for a quick "hello" when you visit the school to pay your child's fees — the same day you get acquainted with the teacher. Again, *make your visit brief.* Just let the principal know who you are, and express your support for the work he or she is doing in the school. That will speak volumes.

Later you get an idea for improving the climate of your school. Call your principal or drop a note to express what you think. Don't blame the principal for the problems you may see; but let the principal know that you are approaching him or her first because you know the key role a principal plays in changing your school.

Several parents had heard disturbing rumors about things that were happening at the high school my daughter attends. A few of them expressed their concern to me. So I invited them to an informal meeting in my home to attempt to lower their anxiety level. There one of the fathers said, "We need to know who these teachers are, and they need to know who we are." He looked at me and said, "Could you set up a meeting?"

The principal gave his okay, and so did the superintendent. Now these parents did not want to meet at the school. They wanted the teachers to be their guests for an evening. So they rented a community building, they brought food in, and they honored the teachers in every way. It was a positive experience of affirming what our teachers are trying to do at the high school. It gave parents a chance to express their concern about some of the fears they held.

I attribute much of that meeting's success to the school principal. His early support paved the way for it all.

Your principal may not give your ideas an enthusiastic response. He or she may have been the victim of so many firebrand critics that he reacts coolly to your ideas. So you try to start changing the climate of your school through the teachers, hoping that you'll sweep the principal along on their coattails. Wrong! You do need to forge a strong partnership with your child's teacher. But be sure the principal is a link in that partnership; bring your ideas for changing the *environment* of the school to him or her first of all. Otherwise you may evoke the principal's worst fears. A recent article in a professional educator's journal said, "If they understand little else, (principals) can quickly sense the power of any loyalties not under their control."[5]

Why add another unnecessary pressure to your principal? Let the principal know that you support his or her work. Become the principal's "idea person"—suggesting methods for constructive change—rather than a "gripe person" who only attacks what is wrong in the school. The principal will appreciate you for it. And you may gain the opportunity to move the moral and spiritual *status quo* of your school.

NOTES

[1]Cliff Schimmels, *How to Help Your Child Survive and Thrive in the Pubic School* (Old Tappan, NJ: Fleming H. Revell Company, 1982), pp. 54-58.

[2]Neil Postman and Charles Weingartner, *Teaching as a Subversive Activity* (New York, NY: Dell Publishing Co., Inc., 1969).

[3]M. Dale Baughman, *The Educator's Handbook of Stories, Quotes, and Humor* (Englewood Cliffs, NJ: Prentice-Hall, 1963), no. 902.

[4]Many parents think that the United States Supreme Court has banned all Bible reading and prayer from the public school. That's not true. The Court issued a series of rulings about twenty years ago which outlawed *mandatory* prayer and Bible reading in the schools; but voluntary prayer and Bible reading are still fully legal. Justice Abe Fortas made the comment that "neither students nor teachers shed their constitutional right to freedom of speech or expression at the schoolhouse gate." But the principal will affect the exercise of that right, by his or her personal attitude toward prayer and Bible reading. If teachers and students sense that the principal frowns on these activities, they will be less likely to do them.

[5]David S. Seeley, "Education Through Partnership," *Educational Leadership*, November 1982, p. 43.

The Curriculum

Imagine the students at your school are a track team. Strong, well-trained athletes. The principal is their coach. The teachers are their pacesetters (every good track team has them). And today they've come to the World Olympics. They've endured the long, grueling days of training; now they're ready to compete with athletes from other teams in ... the race of life.

How well do these trim young athletes run the race? That depends.

It depends on the pacesetters to be sure. And the coach. Not to mention the athletes themselves and their sponsors (that's *you*, Mom and Dad). How well have you supported these young people in their days of training? How much have you helped with the training? That will affect the outcome of the race as much as anything else.

But there's another factor we ought to mention—the training course. That's the cinder track where the athletes have run month after month. How well was it constructed? How fully has it prepared them? How closely does it resemble the track where they will compete for the big prize? Yes, the training course is important. Let's hope it really was a training course, and not just an obstacle course!

I'm talking about your school's curriculum. The curriculum takes your son or daughter around the training laps they need to run, as they prepare for the real "race" of adult living.

Our public schools offer two kinds of curriculum: the written curriculum and the unwritten. Every school has both kinds.

The *written* curriculum is the program of intended learning that is planned and implemented by the school. We find it expressed in textbooks, audiovisuals, and other materials. A parent who enters the school and looks at these materials will get a fairly clear idea of what the school is trying to teach his children. The written curriculum assures you that there is uniformity, organization, and progression in your child's education.

The effectiveness of a school is closely tied to the formal written curriculum. This is why so many states' attorneys general have gotten involved in court cases about curriculum (evolution, sex education, etc.). We will see these test cases for some time to come; they prove how much importance the public attaches to the written curriculum.

The *unwritten* curriculum (also called "the hidden curriculum") is anything that the teacher or students bring into the classroom which helps to shape the learning program or mold the attitude of the class. The unwritten curriculum is not so easily identified as the written curriculum--and therefore not so easy to control. Pupils themselves have a strong role in shaping the unwritten curriculum; we call it "peer pressure."

Let's consider how these two kinds of curriculum affect our children's learning in the public schools.

Unwritten Curriculum

As a parent, I will tend to evaluate the teacher's un-written curriculum in light of my own. If the teacher's underlying ideas and attitudes agree with mine, I'll think she has a good unwritten curriculum; but if they don't, I'll think she's having a negative influence.

Students evaluate a teacher's unwritten curriculum, too. Kids have pretty good "antennas," and when they walk into a new classroom they get an impression of what that teacher's ideas and attitudes are. It's especially easy for them to spot the unwritten curriculum in subject areas such as health, literature, or social studies. They have various ideas about the issues being discussed, and the teacher's own ideas may soon pop up.

The teacher is not just a machine; he doesn't just dispense an objective question followed by an objective answer. He has feeling, attitudes, and ideas of his own. He won't be able to hide them from his students forever. His convictions surely will spin out in any free-wheeling discussion of controversial topics.

Of course, the teacher's unwritten curriculum has two parts—the *intentional* and the *unintentional.* If I am teaching a class, my lectures and conversations with the students will carry some subtle freight that I'm not even aware of. My attitudes and habits are so much a part of me that I don't even realize they are there. But my students will. Just watch a junior high or senior high variety show where a couple of clever kids do impersonations of the teachers. Everyone will roar with laughter—except perhaps the teacher who's being impersonated! He probably never realized he had personal quirks so noticeable that everyone else would recognize them. Those quirks are part of his unintentional hidden curriculum. They may be expressed by physical movements, tone of voice, certain expressions, or a particular attitude or prejudice.

A few teachers have an intentional hidden curriculum. They are trying to change their students' attitudes, in very subtle or very forthright ways. (I had more to say about this in the chapter on "The Teacher and the Principal.")

The Written Curriculum

A school without a written curriculum would be like the ship whose captain found himself in a fog with a broken compass. He sent his first mate to the bow with a sack of potatoes, with orders to throw a potato as far as he could in front of the ship. If they didn't hear a splash, they would turn the ship! The written curriculum is a navigation chart. Your school officials can use it to guide your children to moral and intellectual maturity—avoiding plenty of reefs along the way.

When we speak of written curriculum, we normally mean the textbooks that are used. But it also includes library books, supplementary texts, audiovisuals, field trips—anything that is a part of the planned program of education at your school.

The written curriculum is always changing in response to forces outside the school. For example, most of us look back at the 1950s as a time of stability in our American society; but strong undercurrents of change in the 1950s influenced our public schools in a very significant way. Civil rights agitation, the "Cold War" with the Soviet Union, rapid technological advances in atomic energy and electronics—all of these affected the school curriculum in that decade.

When the Soviet Union sent up Sputnik I in October of 1957, there was an immediate clamor to "catch up with the Russians" in space technology; this brought even more dramatic changes to our public schools. Educators began a drive for math and science courses in our schools. We feared the Soviet Union, and Sputnik confirmed our fears that we had fallen behind the

U.S.S.R., militarily and scientifically. We weren't afraid that we would fail to launch satellites; we were afraid that Russia had better missile technology that would permit her to launch atomic warheads we couldn't shoot down! So there was strong public support for the dramatic shift toward math and science in our public schools.

The federal government granted large sums of money for these changes. Local governments consolidated their schools at a faster rate, because larger schools meant more funds per pupil for staff and equipment.

While math and science were being "beefed up" in our public-school curriculum, subjects such as literature and foreign languages went into retrenchment. After all, how could a course in Latin or medieval English drama help you build a better I.C.B.M.? This trend *away* from the liberal arts began in the 1950s and accelerated in the next two decades.

The big event of the 1960s was the Vietnam War. It created a youth culture that was "turned off" by all the traditional values of our Western society. Teachers felt they couldn't relate to junior high and senior high students anymore; even the "straight" kids burned their draft cards and wore black armbands to school! Boys' hair dropped to shoulder length; peace symbols were plastered everywhere; and the ethical values of young people did an about-face. The public schools made an effort to reach these disenchanted, disaffectioned young people by offering exotic new courses to stimulate their interest. They replaced traditional English literature with electives like "Whodunit?" (a course in popular spy novels) and "Journal-Keeping" (a course in how to write a diary).

In the 1970s, affective education became the "in" thing. Schools offered courses that taught the student how to shape his attitudes and values, rather than imparting a specific block of facts or a measurable skill. Curriculum planners wanted to mold the psyche of their students, rather than the intellect. This change was not demanded by the public (as the technology push of the 1950s was); it was demanded by educational theorists at high levels of academia, who felt such courses would be good for our students.

Some have called the 1970s the "Me Decade," because it placed such strong emphasis on the self. Advertising told us, "Do something nice for yourself"; "You deserve a break today"; and so on. Popular books advised us how to "get in touch with yourself" and "find your center." The 1970s gave us Transcendental Meditation, EST, assertiveness training, and other courses for strengthening the self. So perhaps there was an undercurrent of public support for this change in our schools' curriculum. But I believe most of the impctus for affective education came from the theorists.

Mini-courses were added to schools' curriculum in the 1960s and 1970s. Mini-courses lasted for three, six, or nine weeks of the semester; they dealt with subjects of special interest that did not really warrant a full semester of study. Many parents felt uncomfortable with this trend. They said the mini-courses gave their children a piecemeal education; they preferred the more traditional semester-long or year-long courses. *Phi Delta Kappan* magazine made a recent study of over two hundred schools, and it found a sharp decline in the number of mini-courses offered in every subject area from 1976 to 1981.[1] So innovations in the curriculum aren't always permanent; in fact, most educators will scrap their new ideas if they don't pan out.

The 1980s seem to be giving us three major trends in our curriculum; "back to the basics," computer technology, and minimum competency testing.

Few schools put aside some of the rudimentary courses in reading, grammar, and algebra during the trendy curriculum revisions of the 1970s; most kept these foundational courses. So "back to the basics" sim ply means strengthening the schools' basic courses of instruction. But the bad publicity about the exotic courses of the 1970s aroused a loud public cry to get "back to the basics," and I'm sure our curriculum planners will take a more serious look at this need during the rest of the 1980s.

Schools' performance can be checked with *minimum competency testing*. In other words, they can give students a prescribed test and say, "If you don't make a certain minimum score on this test, you won't graduate." Schools usually give competency tests at various levels such as third grade, sixth grade, ninth grade, and so on. If a student isn't able to pass the competency test for his particular level, he takes remedial training and may be held back for a year.

Minimum competency testing would have been a heresy in the 1960s and early 1970s. Students would have said, "You can't squeeze me into everyone else's mold. I'm unique." In fact, some people still feel these tests are intolerable. But I believe we will see the tests used more frequently in the 1980s. The push for teaching computer technology in our public schools also has strong grass roots support, and every school can afford to buy the equipment. In the late 1970s, computer manufacturers placed a variety of inexpensive, high-capacity microcomputers on the market. Right now you can buy for $1,200 a microcomputer that can do faster calculations and store more information than a $250,000 mainframe computer could in 1968. A second-grade child now has at his disposal the same computer capacity that only the large corporations could afford just fifteen years ago. And the innovations haven't ended. Every month our computer manufacturers give us even better computers for less money.[2]

Though computer technology is a high priority for our public schools in the 1980s, there has been a critical shortage of math and science teachers.[3] Why? Because recent college graduates, who prepared to teach math and science, woke up on graduation day to the fact that the average *starting* pay in industry is 50-70% higher than the average *lifetime* pay a math or science teacher would receive. The salary gap is very wide. And not many people are trained to teach computer science at any price.

We've had such a glut of teachers in recent years that guidance counselors warned young people to avoid careers in education. They didn't think they could get jobs. For a while that was true. But the pendulum is swinging the other way again.

A serious problem is on the horizon. California, Florida, Texas, Indiana, Georgia, North Carolina, Minnesota, Maryland, and other states have imposed more stringent graduation requirements. Most state Departments of Education have mandated the teaching of more math and science; and that has the potential to intensify the shortage of math and science teachers. It will place quite a burden on the curriculum planners of our local schools. They must decide how to offer more math, science, and computer courses without qualified teachers. No doubt, financial incentive will be offered for those already teaching to retrain in the area of math or science.

According to the *ERS Bulletin,* only eight states do not have a serious or critical shortage of math or science teachers. Parents may not realize there is a shortage because their school board may be filling a vacancy with a poorly trained or untrained teacher until they can find someone who's qualified to teach that class. State Departments of Education can issue permits for an uncertified or undercertified person to teach a given class, if there is no one else to take that position.

In the 1980s, parents want to see our schools move "back to basics" and teach their children how to use computers. This doesn't mean they no longer care about other aspects of the curriculum; it simply means that these two areas are "front burner" concerns right now.

Priorities for Our Curriculum

Each year the *Phi Delta Kappan* magazine commissions a Gallup Poll on public education. In 1982, more than one-third of the educators who responded to this poll felt that our schools' curriculum should be changed to meet today's needs. But how should it be changed? That's not so easy to answer.

This question forces us to think seriously about what we want to accomplish in our schools. What should be our priorities? How should our curriculum reflect these priorities? And how can we determine whether our schools are meeting these priorities?

Tough questions! Yet they get to the heart of curriculum planning in our schools.

One of the first priorities, obviously, is to teach our children the "three R's" of pioneer days. The "back to basics" movement has induced teachers and parents to give more attention to teaching children these vital skills. But what about students who learn the "basics" for that year by November? Teachers must not focus so intently on teaching slow learners that they ignore kids who learn the "basics" easily.

First-grade teachers feel compelled to teach their students to read. And why not? Parents expect it and so do the children. When a student has reading difficulties in later years, someone's sure to say, "Who was his first-grade teacher, anyway? He must not have had a very good start!" So a first-grade teacher feels under more pressure than a fifth-grade teacher. She expects to give all her children the basics of reading and writing that year. She believes that if she doesn't, her pupils are going to fail in life. That's a heavy load to bear. Yet a first-grade teacher often will strap that load to her back.

How much of the "basics" must a child know to continue his education? We need to resolve this question in the 1980s; it's top priority in our curriculum planning. Minimum competency testing will focus the attention of the academic community on this area.

In some parts of the country, you will find specialized courses because of a regional interest. For example, high schools in Colorado might offer snow-skiing courses as part of their physical education program. Schools in California (where there's a strong interest in health foods) might offer a course in herbal cookery.

One of my professors at Ball State University used to go every summer to teach in a school for Eskimos on one of the islands off the Alaskan coast. A requirement for graduation from that elementary school was that every student had to know how to do routine maintenance on an outboard motor. Why? Because it was a fishing island, and every person who lived there had to be able to survive on the high seas. Every child needed to know how to get his boat motor started again if it stalled.

Here and there, schools have begun courses for helping the children of divorced parents to cope with the turmoil in their lives.[4] School administrators must deal with these problems in the affective area before they can teach anything in the cognitive area. One administrator said:

The upheaval in these children's lives spills over into the classrooms and often into the guidance and administrative offices with a wide range of problems, from poor academic performance to increased social and behavioral problems.[5]

I remember a very clear example of this. About seven years ago, I was working in a school that created a "split room" to relieve the overflow in the second and third grades. A teacher agreed to teach the class, provided she and the principal could choose the students who would go into the split room. They picked the students who seemed to be independent learners, who needed the least supervision. Later in the year, that teacher said, "You know, I realized an interesting thing the other day. I have twenty-eight students in that class; twenty-seven of them have always lived in the same home with the same mother and father. Only one comes from a divorced family."

That same year, our junior high school had a program for students with learning deficiencies. The students were selected on the basis of how they had performed in the classroom; they were what many people would call "poor achievers." There were thirty-two students in that class, and thirty of them had come from broken homes.

The home is not the sole factor in determining how well a child learns at school. But I think we can't ignore the correlation. And neither do the school administrators who are starting special courses for children with problems at home, such as divorce or alcoholism. These students have a significant amount of stress, and that stress is sure to affect their overall learning.

So you see, your school could add a wide variety of courses to its curriculum—depending on the needs that you and/or your teachers feel your children have. The following chart shows how our public-school curriculum has changed over the past three hundred years.[6] Notice what's been added and what's been deleted:

A Glance at Curriculum Expansion by State Mandate

1675	*1775*	*1875*	*1975*
Reading	Reading	Reading	Reading
Writing	Writing	Writing	Writing
Bible	Arithmetic	Arithmetic	Arithmetic
	Spelling	Spelling	Spelling

Bible	Conduct	Character
	Geography	Education
	History	Narcotics/
	Art	Drugs
	Music	Health/
	Physical	Nutrition
	Education	History
		Patriotism
		Current
		Events
		Art
		Music
		Science
		Safety
		Manners/
		Morals
		Sex
		Education
		Industrial
		Shops
		Commercial
		Consumer
		Languages
		Physical
		Education

This gives you some idea of the various demands that have been placed upon the public-school curriculum. It also reflects the fact that our schools are now expected to teach manners, morals, and values that once were the exclusive duty of the parents.

How Parents Influence the Curriculum

We parents already influence the curriculum of our public schools, whether we realize it or not. Many courses of instruction were added to our schools' curriculum because parents financed them.

The push for computer training is a good case in point. Parents raise money for computers in every way imaginable. P.T.A.s are selling candy, cheese, and sausage; businesses are donating money; parents are donating T.V. sets to serve as the video screens.

This is one way parents influence the curriculum—by financing new courses. Schools added mechanical drawing, home economics, driver's education, athletics, marching band, and other subjects to their regimen when parents purchased the hardware. When parents felt a need, they bought the equipment to address that need.

Another way you can influence the curriculum is by serving on the panel that revives curriculum plans. School administrators see the value of having parents help to review the schools' curriculum from time to time. Principals often arrange special meetings of parents and teachers for this specific purpose; and if you're on friendly terms with your principal, you might suggest that he or she do this. A professional journal recently said:

Teachers in partnerships with parents are accountable to them for guiding the learning of their children. They gain authority from this relationship, and they need not be bashful about using it, as long as it genuinely reflects parents' values rather than professional values and interests clothed in "the best interests of the child."[7]

Teachers or principals who feel insecure might not enjoy this kind of cooperative process. They might prefer to keep parents at arm's length. So approach your school officials with tact; be sensitive to their feelings. If they hesitate to bring you into the curriculum-planning process, don't be pushy. You can still influence the curriculum in other ways that will not arouse their hostilities.

66

Mature educators will welcome your input. They are eager to know what you expect of them. They would rather share the responsibility for curriculum-planning with you—the "consumer" they serve—than try to wing it alone. J. Cy Rowell, associate professor of religious education at Texas Christian University, points out that you have five basic rights as a parent[8]:

1. *The right to be informed about your child's teacher.* If you're not given information about the teacher, seek it out. How's she teaching your child to read, for example? Is she using phonics? Linguistics? Sight-reading? Why is that particular method being used? What does she do with the other students when a few are in a reading group? Visit the classroom and find out.

2. *The right to be informed about the curriculum.* You need to know what courses your child is taking, and why. Even in an elementary school, the curriculum can change from year to year. Your friends may not know what their children are being taught, but you should. It's the only way you can intelligently aid the teacher in your child's education. Is there a curriculum guide? Is it policed? Is it representative of what actually is taught?

3. *The right to be informed about official school policies.* What are the school's policies about discipline in the classroom? About riding the school bus? About class attendance? As you move from one school district to another, you'll run into differences in the school policies. Know what the school expects of your child, so that you don't place him in unnecessary conflict with the school. At the beginning of the year, the school may hand out a brochure that explains any special policies they have. You ought to read it! And ask questions if you are still wondering about any aspect of the school's policy.

4. *The right to influence administrative decisions.* This does not mean that parents have the right to *dictate* what school officials do. But you do have the right

to express your views about what happens in your schools, in any legitimate way. Some educators ask parents to help them review the resumes of prospective teachers, and indicate which ones they feel should be hired. That's an innovative idea! I doubt that many administrators will plunge into that very soon. But they would like to share the responsibility for the poor choices that will be made now and then.

5. *The right to influence school policy.* Rowell says, "Parents and the general public have traditionally been told that they can influence policy in only two ways—by electing school board members and speaking at school board meetings. While parents have been known to 'clean house' in school board elections and have indeed spoken out at board meetings, the inherent flaw in this historic style of influencing policy is it leads to polarizing confrontation, to say nothing of its being slow."[9] You can talk with your administrators by telephone, you can visit them at their offices, you can strike up casual conversations with them at the grocery store—there are any number of ways you can influence their decisions outside the rigidly official process of elections and board meetings. Why not try it?

The public-school curriculum will never remain static. Our society is changing too rapidly to let it. As our society changes, people expect our schools to change along with it; that compels us to rethink our curriculum nearly every year. Yet change comes slowly. For the most part, principals don't want to stir up a lot of hostility in their community with avante garde curriculum programs. So they take plenty of time to test the winds of change; they make sure they know which way the winds are blowing before they rearrange the curriculum.

By the way, the principal is the primary agent of change so far as the curriculum is concerned. He or she is the one who is finally responsible for the way that school is organized and for the academic standards it

68

keeps. He or she may consult parents, teachers, and the pupils themselves about ideas for curriculum change; but the principal usually has the final word to keep or delete a course. The principal coordinates the academic program of the school. He or she calls together parents, teachers, school board members, and any others who wish to discuss the academic climate of the school. A wise principal wants to hear and evaluates what these people have to say!

I think most parents who examine the academic climate of their school would agree on two things: (1) There should be a thorough instruction in basic academic skills, so that any student who is capable may have the opportunity to do further study. (2) There must be periodic adjustments in the curriculum of the school to meet the demands of the job marketplace. This means that Christian parents should be willing to heed the wind of change, when a moral issue is not involved.

You can influence your school's curriculum by getting involved in your local P.T.A. As I pointed out, many P.T.A.s and other parents' organizations are helping to shape their curriculum right now by raising money for select programs. But the P.T.A. has other ways of influencing the school program: It has a powerful voice before the school board. If your group feels a certain course should be added to the curriculum, the president or some other representative can plead your case before the board with more clout than any individual parent. The P.T.A. has skillful lobbyists in Congress and the state legislature, too. So if you must change the law in order to change your curriculum, the P.T.A. is in a good position to do exactly that.

Why Get Involved?

If we have "public schools," what makes them public? Our tax dollars?

Parents must answer with a resounding "No!"

Public schools are "public" because the public is involved. If the public is *not* involved, then all we have here are government schools. Parents and other taxpayers should take an active role in their schools. And school administrators, for the most part, want us to do that.

You may not always be able to identify a problem in your school's curriculum. You may not be able to say how your child should learn to read. But at the very least you should be able to say, "Something's wrong here," when you detect a problem in the curriculum. By all means, get involved in the planning.

NOTES

[1]John Guenther and Robert Ridgway, "Where Have All the Mini-Courses Gone?" *Phi Delta Kappan,* September 1982, p. 69. The decline in mini-courses ranged from 45% to 100% (total elimination of the mini-courses).

[2]For further information about the impact of computer training on public-school curriculum, see Silva Pheng, Anna Monardo, Lorraine Hopping, and Peggy Gladstone, "Survey of the States," *Electronic Learning,* November-December 1982, pp. 62-71.

[3]*ERS Bulletin,* February 1982, pp. 6, 7.

[4]Lynne Ames, "For Children of the Divorced, A Course on How to Cope," *The New York Times Fall Review of Education,* November 14, 1982, pp. 19, 20.

[5]*Ibid.,* p. 19.

[6]David H. Paynter, *Must Our Schools Die?* (Portland, OR: Multnomah Press, 1980), p. 133.

[7]David S. Seeley, "Education Through Partnership," *Educational Leadership,* November 1982, p. 43.

[8]J. Cy Rowell, "The Five Rights of Parents," *Phi Delta Kappan,* February 1981, pp. 441-443.

[9]*Ibid.,* p. 443.

Three Touchy Subjects

Since we're thinking about the curriculum, let's take a look at three of the most controversial subjects taught in public schools today: evolution, sex education, and values clarification. These three subjects are most likely to cause friction between parents and teachers, if they are offered at your school.

At a natural point in a young person's life, he may respect the teachers' authority more than mom or dad's. In the young person's rebellion against parental authority, he turns to the next natural source—the schoolmaster—for the answers to life's questions. Educators have always assumed that a teacher acts *in loco parentis* (Latin, "in place of the parent"). In other words, the teacher supports and reinforces the values a parent has taught at home. But this concept does not hold sway in the 1980s as it did one generation ago.

Today, many teachers feel free to persuade pupils to their own values, rather than reinforcing the parents' values. This makes the "touchy subjects" touchier than ever. When the teacher promotes her own views on evolution, sex education, or any other subject, she rouses the ire of parents in her community. This brings Christian parents into the battle. And it creates a hostile adversary relationship between parents and teachers, which makes learning even more difficult for the child.

Let's try to head off that conflict before it begins.

Evolution

The British scientist Charles Darwin is credited for first expounding the theory of evolution, in the mid-1800s. Scientific journals had hinted at the idea long before, but Darwin was the first to marshal a long chain of biological evidence in support of it. His 1859 book entitled *The Origin of the Species* set forth the basic theory: That all forms of life now on the earth have evolved (or developed) from simpler forms of life.

Let's retrace the development of this concept, because it will help us understand why there is so much controversy about it today.

Darwin's book, *The Origin of the Species* grew out of a round-the-world tour that he had made on the *H.M.S. Beagle.* On that tour, he collected a vast amount of botanical evidence which showed there was a great diversity in the creatures of this world. But Darwin also found many parallel features in the various species of plants or animals. These parallel features led Darwin to suggest that animals had evolved from simpler forms to more complex ones—and that plants had evolved in the same way.

When Darwin published his book in Great Britain, his theory was mainly a matter for the scientific community to discuss. It was an academic piece. But the topic broke into the public forum when essayist T.H. Huxley picked up the cause of evolution and took it one step further. Huxley said that if simple animals did evolve to more complex animals, it would be reasonable to assume that apes and other anthropoids (manlike creatures) had evolved from lower forms of life. Huxley began promoting his idea on the lecture circuit, asserting that man was just a more sophisticated kind of animal. That's when the church entered the debate. Huxley had some very heated public debates with the church leaders of Great Britain. Ever since that time, evolution has been a touchy issue for Christians around the world.

One point that Christians haven't discussed a great deal is whether evolution is really a theory. I feel we ought to make the distinction between a *theory* and a *hypothesis*. Walter Brown points out that when you start researching the origins of the planets, or even the origins of man, you have to formulate a "working model" of how things might have happened.[1] All of your evidence has been destroyed! So you must form a "working model" and ask, "Does the world as we know it today resemble what might have come out of that model?" Scientists call such a "working model" a *hypothesis*.

... Only if you get an overwhelming amount of evidence for that model do you begin to call it a *theory*.

... And only when you've tested it in the laboratory time and again, under various conditions, and proven it true do you call it a *natural law*.

Biology textbooks a generation ago did not call Darwin's idea "the theory of evolution"; they called it "the evolutionary hypothesis." Since then, even Christians have labeled it a "theory"; but I think the distinction still ought to be made. The weight of evidence just isn't there. The creation of the universe isn't the sort of thing you can recreate and test in a laboratory. You can't possibly retrace several million years of reproduction to see if evolution really takes place. Scientists have used fruit flies, which reproduce every few days, to study several hundred thousand generations to see if any evolutionary mutations occur. But even with fruit flies they can't get enough reproductive generations to show whether Darwin's idea is correct. And, after thousands of generations, fruit flies still produce fruit flies!

By no stretch of the imagination should evolution be called a "law of nature." It should not even be called a theory. It is still a *hypothesis*—a scientist's "working model" of how he supposes complex forms of life arose on this earth.

Darwin said that the chemical "building blocks" of life were made by accident in the primordial soup of the barren earth, billions of years ago. He believed these chemicals then combined by accident to make the first one-celled organisms which lived in the oceans. Then, he said, these one-celled animals developed into more complex animals—eels and fish, etc. Over many millions of years, some of these animals developed lungs and land legs; they became amphibians, which could live on land or in water. Some amphibians evolved into reptiles, which lived solely on dry land. Some reptiles evolved into marsupials (having some characteristics of reptiles and some characteristics of mammals); then some marsupials evolved into mammals, warm-blooded animals that bore their young alive. Some mammals developed into apes and others developed into primitive man. (Darwin did *not* believe that man evolved from apes; he believed men and apes developed from the same branch of the biological family tree.)

As you can see, this is a fairly complicated theory. (Just summarizing for you is complicated!) But many scientists and educators now accept this as the standard explanation of how man came to live on the earth.

In what school course do you suppose your child will

first encounter the theory of evolution? A science class? High school biology? You may be surprised to learn that evolution may first crop up in *social studies.*

When young people study world history, their textbook may have a chapter dealing with early man. There you may find artists' renditions of prehistoric man with receding forehead—a "missing link" between the ape and modern man.

The public schools are not the only forum where evolution is discussed, either. I can pick up an issue of *National Geographic* magazine, for example, and read comments subtly promoting the theory of evolution. Magazines, newspapers, TV documentaries, and other media sources put the idea of evolution across in a very subtle and effective way. They often imply that evolution is the only valid explanation of man's beginnings. In recent decades, evolution has always had the edge over "creation" in public-school science and social studies curriculum. But Creationists are pressing school officials, through the courts, to give an equal hearing to both views in the school classroom. So far Creationists are losing the battle. Yet we can be sure to hear more of this controversy in the years ahead.

Public school curriculum planners got mixed in the creation-evolution debate during the infamous 1925 trial of John T. Scopes, a high school biology teacher in Dayton, Tennessee. The prosecuting attorney, William Jennings Bryan, insisted that Mr. Scopes was teaching that man evolved from monkeys. So newspaper reporters called it the "Monkey Trial."

Bryan cited the book of Genesis as proof that man could not have evolved from the apes. He affirmed the Biblical accounts, which says that God created the first man from the dust of the ground. But the defending attorney, Clarence Darrow, declared that Mr. Scopes taught only what was based on solid scientific evidence. Darrow said that the Bible would not stand up under critical scrutiny. In proving it, he called Mr.

Bryan himself to the witness stand and gave him a grueling interrogation about the Bible.

The court found Mr. Scopes guilty of violating Tennessee law, which prohibited the teaching of evolution; he was fined $100. But a high court overturned this ruling and rescinded the fine. Mr. Scopes kept his job. Eventually, Tennessee's law against teaching evolution was struck down. But fundamentalists look back on the Scopes trial as a landmark test of their belief in the infallibility of God's Word. This is one reason why evolution is still such a touchy issue for all Christians. The Scopes trial left the taste of defeat in our mouths. Subconsciously, we feel a duty to vindicate Bryan and all the other fervent Christians who have opposed evolution in the courtrooms of our land—and have lost.

But there are more important reasons to oppose the teaching of evolution alone. First, we should realize that a number of notable scientists believe the Biblical account of creation has more scientific merit than evolution.[2] James H. Jauncey says, "There are a great number of biologists who at least tentatively believe in evolution but who nevertheless are active members of Christian churches and find no problem at all. The general attitude is that, even if evolution were proved to be true, instead of making God unnecessary, it would merely show that this was the method God used."[3] Dozens of books and magazine articles by reputable biologists assert that the evolutionary hypothesis is not valid but the creation account is valid. So why should evolution be taught by itself? Why shouldn't creation be taught along with it? Why shouldn't our students have a chance to examine scientific evidence for *both* explanations of man's origins on this planet?

Some time ago, I was talking with a ninth-grade student who'd found the evolutionary account of early man in his world history textbook. I asked him whether his textbooks presented the Bible account of creation as an alternative view of man's origins. He said, "No, it didn't. The book only gave us the scientific view." You see, this young man already believes that anything which comes from the Bible cannot be substantiated by science. But that's not true. Yet we have a mountain of scientific proof for creation—and that mountain gets higher every day!

This is the first reason why I oppose the teaching of evolution alone: It is not sound educational practice to lift up one hypothesis as the only feasible explanation of an event—especially when so many scientists question that hypothesis.

Second, we should realize that the theory of evolution casts grave doubts upon man's relationship to God. If man evolved through a complex series of random mutations, how can he respect God's claim to moral authority over his life? The Bible says that God's authority grows out of the fact that He created us. If He didn't create us, a major tenet of the Bible's teaching is false, and the rest of the Bible's teachings become suspect.[4] Evolution implies that "man is not 'fallen' or sinful, as Genesis teaches. An evolved animal has no need of a Savior."[5]

Are you concerned about the teaching of evolution in your public schools? Then think about the implications and consequences of this teaching. Note that the evolutionary hypothesis affects the foundation stones of your theology. Until the Christian community realizes this, we are less likely to change school policy about the teaching of evolution.

Many evangelical Christians believe that *both* evolution and creation should be presented to our public-school students. They say these views should be given equal time in the classroom, presented as *conflicting and mutually excludable philosophies*. They believe the theory of evolution contradicts the Bible account of creation, and they see no way to reconcile them. But they think their children should understand *both* views of man's origins, in order to have a complete education. They think the public-school classroom is the best place to discuss both views.

The Arkansas State Legislature passed a law to do this very thing in the 1982-1983 school year, but courts overturned the law. The American Civil Liberties Union (A.C.L.U.) mounted a strong drive to win this case. Evangelical leaders planned to appeal the decision to the United States Supreme Court, so we have not heard the last of this equal-time concept.[6]

But I must confess that I disagree with my evangelical friends at this point. I believe non-Christian science teachers who are biased toward evolution would have difficulty presenting both creation and evolution in their classes. Even if a state mandated equal time for both views, the non-Christian teacher's personal bias would come through very strongly. His "hidden curriculum" would still be there. So the net effect would still be to discredit the Bible in the eyes of his students. While he might give equal time to teaching creation, he would still bend his students' belief away from creation in a very subtle way. I would prefer to see both issues given equal treatment in whatever textbook is used. This would tend to promote open discussion of both sides.

Ideally, I would like to see each classroom have a Christian teacher who would approach this subject from two vantage points: (1) by reading and discussing Genesis 1–3 and a text about creation science—that is, the physical evidence for creation, and (2) by reading and discussing a text about evolution. I would not want the teacher to *promote* evolution, but he should educate his pupils about it, as well as about creation. I don't feel this approach should be state mandated. It should be purely voluntary, something that a teacher is allowed to do if he feels inclined. In that environment, where the teacher is not compelled to teach one view or the other, I believe the Bible account of creation will stand on its own merits without any help.

Well, what can you do about the teaching of evolution in your school? Try to make sure that your teacher won't be antagonistic to the Christian views you instill at home. There's no guarantee that he'll *support* your values; but is he's attacking them, you should press for an open class discussion.

Ask your local church to have a series of lessons on creation. Such a course could extend over three or four days, starting with a film about creation (the Moody Science Series has excellent material along this line), and continuing with a guest speaker who is knowledgeable on this subject. You may live near a Christian college or university that has a teacher who could lead this series. Look around you; the resources are there. Your church could provide a clear, intelligent discussion of the scientific evidence for creation, geared to junior high and senior high students. Give these students an opportunity to hear the other side of the story, which they may not hear in the public classroom.

Get appointed to a textbook adoption committee for your school. That's where you can make a long-range impact on the problem. (See my chapter on "Choosing the Textbooks.") Let's suppose you are on a textbook committee considering four biology texts. And let's suppose that all four books are acceptable to you as a Christian, except for their teaching of evolution. You could propose that the school add a supplementary textbook to the course, or place in the school library a book describing the Bible account of creation from a scientific point of view.

The concept of evolution will be with us for a long time. There's no way to prove evolution, but there seems no way to dismiss it, either. We Christians would be lulling ourselves into a false sense of security if we said, "Well, evolution's not all it was cracked up to be. Let's ignore it, and it will go away." It won't go away, and we must respond to it.

We are too shy to talk with our non-Christian friends about creation and evolution, because we think we're hanging by a scientific thread. We just don't realize how thin the evidence is for evolution! Evolution does not stand on rock-solid evidence; in fact, there is far more scientific evidence for creation than for evolution. So we should stand by our beliefs without any embarrassment.

Sex Education

Sex education is fairly common in junior high and high school curricula now. Most schools offer something on this subject, though the program varies from school to school. In one system, it may consist of a few days' instruction in the physiology of sex in a biology class. In another, it may deal with the proper care of the sexual organs, or as part of a course on health and personal hygiene. In another system, it may take the form of a full-blown course in human sexuality which deals with intercourse, venereal disease, and sexual morality, among other things.

Here is how Peggy Brick teaches sex education at Dwight Morrow High School in Englewood, New Jersey. It's an eight-week unit in an introductory course on behavioral science:

We begin the unit with a sex knowledge survey — seventy questions directed at common misconceptions about sex. Students have two days to find the correct answers from any source, including parents and teachers. Then, with even the coolest ones humbled, we discuss the answers fully. We read and evaluate the controversial comic book, *Ten Heavy Facts About Sex* (Gordon: 1973). We have a hilarious (and for some, embarrassing) time listing slang words under proper sex terms posted in the room — an effective technique for "desensitizing" these words and preparing students for responsible discussion. We also embellish the bulletin board with the "lines" people use to seduce members of the opposite sex (Gordon: 1979).[7]

This does not describe my school's sex education program. Does it describe yours? This teacher takes words from the rest room walls and puts them on the bulletin board and chalkboard, embarrassing some students, so that she can "desensitize" the words—i.e., make them acceptable for classroom conversation. (I think she has a very strong "hidden curriculum" here.) She also uses values clarification exercises so the students will examine their sexual mores and decide whether they should change. At the end of the unit, she gives them another survey to see how their attitudes and knowledge have changed as a result of the study. She says, "Significantly, many still feel reluctant to discuss sex with their parents, which reflects the fact that communication between parents and teenagers is not adequate for sex education to be left to parents."[8]

I'm sure there's some truth to what Ms. Brick says. Some parents don't have enough knowledge of sex; those who have the knowledge aren't inclined to teach it to their children; and many parents have neither the knowledge nor the inclination to teach it. Is it the best remedy, then, to turn sex education over to the public schools?

We've long had public-school courses in hygiene. There children learn how to care for the feet, their eyes, their ears, and so on. That's only natural. So it's just as natural to teach young people about sex, right?

But there's an important difference. Caring for your feet, eyes, and ears will involve no moral decisions. But moral decisions are always involved in our handling of sex. There's no "hidden curriculum" about teaching you how to wash behind your ears. But there certainly can be a "hidden curriculum" about teaching high school students how to use contraceptives.

Evangelical leaders question the value of these sex

education courses. They feel that these programs make promiscuity more widespread, and abstinence rare. When sex is discussed even in the classroom, they say, our young people feel that intercourse should be the "meat and potatoes" of life rather than the "caviar." Opal Moore notes:

In 1971, four years after the New York City School Board inaugurated "family life" education, including sex education (elementary grades through high school), the label "CYESIS" was chosen for six special schools. "CYESIS" means pregnancy. The schools were needed to take care of more than 1,700 pregnant girls in grades seven through twelve. Another twelve hundred pregnant girls were expected to continue attending classes in their regular schools. In addition, an estimated fifty thousand girls had obtained legal abortions in the previous year and a half. What went wrong? Some educators thought the program wasn't sufficiently implemented; some students claimed they needed *more* information about sexuality and the prevention of pregnancy.[9]

Kentucky and Maryland have mandated sex education courses in their public schools. Since those laws went into effect, pregnancies have increased in Kentucky by nine percent and in Maryland by twenty-four and a half percent. The number of abortions has increased in Kentucky by eighty-six percent and in Maryland by 228 percent. So while the proponents of sex education tell us these classes will control promiscuity and its related health problems, the statistics do not seem to support that.[10]

A New Jersey law mandating that sex education be taught in public schools was upheld last week by a 7-0 vote in the state supreme court.

The court said the mandate, which goes into effect in

September 1983 for grades 5 to 12, does not impinge on religious freedom or establish "secular humanism" as a religion, as critics had contended. The law, it said, allows students to leave class if their parents or guardians requested it on religious grounds. About 40 percent of the state's districts are teaching sex education now.[11]

Clearly, our young people need to understand how to become mature adults, who express their sexuality in a mature way. Our young people need some type of sex education. Where is the best place to provide sex education? What should we teach? And what is the best way to teach it?

I believe our public schools do a good job of presenting the physiological aspects of sex education. Our high school biology teachers and health teachers help our young people understand how their sex organs are developing. They have marvelous visual materials—filmstrips, models, and illustrated texts—that were not available one decade ago. And so our girls are more likely to understand their menstrual periods; our boys are more likely to understand their "wet dreams"; all are more likely to grasp the basic facts of how their bodies function sexually.

But our public schools, our homes, and society in general are not doing such a good job of teaching them *responsibility* for their sexual behavior. This explains the rapid rise in teenage pregnancy and venereal disease. Our public-school teachers too often don't give young people a solid ethical base for sexual decisions. They don't provide any standard for deciding what is right and what is wrong. That is a grave shortcoming.

As Christian parents, we care about the values being taught to our children in public schools. Luke 17:2 says, "It would be better for him (a teacher) if a millstone were hung around his neck and he were thrown into the sea, than that he should cause one of these little ones to stumble." Sometimes educators aren't too careful about the psychological or moral effects of what they teach. But parents care. Christian parents ought to take action, if they find the school's sex education program—or any other program—causes their young people to stumble into immorality. Here are some things you might do, if you find that your school's sex education program is morally harmful:

Ask school officials to require the parents' signature for taking sex education. Some states, such as California, have the reverse as their policy; students are automatically allowed to register for sex education unless their parents *disapprove* in writing. This places the student in an awkward situation. I taught in a school in which the teacher sent a note home by the students when the sex education unit was about to be taught. The note explained what the course was about, and required the parents' signature before the student was allowed to enroll.

Ask school officials to make sex education an elective class. If the class violates your religious convictions, your child should not be required to take it in order to graduate.

Ask school officials to describe the course materials in detail when they write to you about the sex education program. The school ought to set aside a couple of hours one afternoon for the parents to screen this material, in the classroom, before it is used. This is the best way for Christian parents to know beforehand whether they're making a wise decision in letting their children attend the class. The school should allow you to see the film, review the books, and talk with the teacher who will be leading the class. A great deal of community controversy could be avoided, if a school took this step before the class began.

If controversial issues such as abortion will be discussed in the class, ask school officials to allow equal time for the presentation of opposing views. You might be able to suggest a capable speaker to present the Christian view, if your teacher plans to espouse the secular view.

Ask to observe the class in session. If the school's advance information about the class is accurate—and it should be—the principal and teacher should have no qualms about letting you observe the class in action someday. If they refuse to let you observe, or if they become hostile, you should investigate the situation further and perhaps withdraw your child from the program.

Talk with your own children; find out what they are learning in the sex education class. This is where you learn what "hidden curriculum" they're getting, as well as the written curriculum. Ask what they do in the classroom. Ask what topics they have discussed as a group or privately with the teacher. Ask what textbooks and audio-visuals are being used (even if you've already gotten a preview).

If you must lodge a complaint, be sure you know what you're talking about. Check out the facts before you go to the principal's office. Then go as an inquirer rather than an accuser. The principal still may think you're narrow-minded. But you are a constituent of the school, and you have the privilege to inquire about what is being taught there.

Consider starting a sex education course at your church. Most denominations have produced some sort of curriculum material for sexuality education. You may think some of it is too liberal (morally) or too vividly illustrated. But ask your pastor whether your church has such material and whether you could have a session in sexuality education for interested students and parents.

Steve Clapp, director of C-4 Resources of Champaign, IL, says that young people who attend church are just as prone to be sexually active as other young people. So churches need to teach their young people about sex and sexual ethics. We can't just assume that they are absorbing this information along the way. Mr. Clapp recommends that each church have a course in sex education for *their youth.* So would I. At your church, the older folks may fear that talking about sex will promote promiscuous sexual activity among teens. (They need to remember that our children are absorbing some of the world's ideas about sexuality in newspapers, magazines, theater marquees, TV, and many other more subtle ways.) You still could have a sex education program for the parents, and let the information "filter down" to the youth through them. The parents might feel uncomfortable talking about sex at first, but, once the ice is broken, this kind of teaching becomes easier.

About six years ago, my wife and I were teaching a high school Sunday-school class. The pastor gave me a package and said, "Here's something you might be interested in." It was a set of tapes by Charlie Shedd, lectures he'd given before a high school student body about sex, dating, and other teen concerns. Dr. Shedd dealt with subjects that were quite controversial, including masturbation. But we used those tapes as discussion-starters for about three months, and we had excellent results.

Near the end of the series, my wife and I divided the class into girls and boys for some special discussions.... I took the girls and she took the boys! I intended to tell those girls about certain aspects of the male's physical response and prepare them for boys' "come-on" lines. The boys already knew all of that. Likewise, my wife wanted to share some things with the boys about the girls' physical makeup and special physical needs, which the girls didn't need to hear. (She said it was interesting to see how intently those fellows studied the floor as she spoke!)

During the three-month period, not one of the teens made any public comment about what we were discussing in the class. There was no controversy in the church. There was no drop-off in youth attendance. I believe the parents had confidence in us and raised no qualms about our teaching the young people about sex. The *program* is not the only factor to consider when your church has a sex education series for teens. Also consider who will be teaching the program. They must be trustworthy.

Be on guard for any church-sponsored sex education program that involves leaders from Planned Parenthood and other organizations that promote liberal attitudes toward premarital sex and abortion. Evangelical Christian parents should not let their children be taught by "authorities" who take a liberal (even a neutral) moral stance. The *morality* of sex is a vital part of church-sponsored sex education.

The ideal sex education program in a local church would be led by a youth minister or someone else who

... is Scripturally sound,

... has good rapport with teenagers,

... is trusted by the parents of the congregation, and

... has thorough knowledge of sex and sexuality.

One of my pastor friends has such a situation: A member of his congregation is a nurse at the local hospital, a dedicated Christian lady who teaches the LaMaze Method for pregnant women. She feels very comfortable talking before a group of people about the physiology and morality of sex. So she's had several question-and-answer sessions with their youth.

Formal classes on Wednesday night, during the Sunday-school hour, or some other time during the week provide a convenient way for the church to teach young people about sexual morality. Again, I would advise you to look around for the best local Christian resource speaker. (A prophet may be without honor in his own country, so outside speakers may be more effective with young people than someone from your own congregation.) If there's no one in your congregation who can deal with this subject, how about a professor from a local Christian college? A Christian nurse from the local hospital? A staff worker with Youth for Christ or Young Life? All sorts of dedicated Christian leaders are available, if you'll look for them. It would be tragic if your church failed to offer a sex education course simply because you did not have the right leaders.

On the other hand, I would not advise you to plunge ahead with a sex education course in your church if several of the parents are opposed to it. Sex education ought not to be a divisive issue for your church. If you let it become divisive, you will destroy more than you build through sex education.

If you can't have a course in sex education, at least assemble a small library of Christian books on sexuality. That library might best be kept in the youth room in your church. There the materials will be much more widely used than if they are hidden away somewhere in the dark recesses of the general church library. Teens will go to books for information on this subject. It is a nonthreatening way to get the basic facts of sex and sexual morals across to your young people.

Well, what should our young people be taught about sex? I can't detail all of the information here, of course, it's beyond the scope of what I am trying to do in this book. But let me rough out an outline of what I feel our young people ought to be getting from sex education:

First, they should be taught the basic facts of physiology related to sex—how the sex organs come to maturity, how they function, how they should be cared for, etc. Most public-school health courses do a good job of imparting this knowledge, as I pointed out earlier.

Second, we need to explain the emotional dynamics of sex. Girls should know that teenage boys are sexually aggressive. Boys should know their biological urge is strong, but they can control it. For example, if a boy is visiting his girlfriend's home and her parents are away, he may get aroused to the point that he says, "Let's 'go all the way.'" But if the girl says, "I think I just heard my folks pull in the driveway," his urge will stop on a dime!

Boys use "lines" to get girls to agree to sexual intercourse; but girls use "lines" to attract boys, too. Let's prepare teens to handle those "lines."

Third, we should discuss the consequences of premarital intercourse. These consequences can be much more serious for girls than for boys, but both get hurt. Boys are no longer bound to marry girls who get pregnant. So pregnant girls must deal with their pregnancy in one way or another, any of which is painful and traumatic.

Fourth, we should help young people realize that sex is never a proof of love. A survey of one high school showed that the girls were afraid to have a fourth date with a boy. It was an unspoken rule that if you went on a fourth date with a boy you were expected to have intercourse. So the girls in that school had a dilemma. They thought, "If I avoid having sex and continue to date the same boy, the kids around school will think I'm having sex with him anyway. So why not do it?" Peer pressure can exert a powerful influence on our teenagers to engage in sex.

Beyond this, we should train parents to deal with the sexual questions of young children.

Dr. Sol Gordon, director of the Institute for Family Research and Education at Syracuse University, talks to many parents' groups about sex education. He says the question that preschoolers ask their parents most often is, "What does _______ mean?" (Referring to some street term for intercourse.) The child, at that point in his life, does not need or want a lengthy explanation. A brief, simple, unemotional explanation will most often satisfy the curiosity of the moment, without causing any guilt that would stifle future questions or discussion. The parent should simply explain that Christians don't use that word. Though the child hears other children use it, he shouldn't. That's usually enough. You don't need to explain intercourse in great detail for a preschooler; he has used these words innocently, without knowing what they mean. You need to be an askable parent. Your child should know that he can come back and ask you about sex when he's really ready to learn.

It's pretty obvious that many parents just don't know the answers to many questions about sex. If a young person asked you, "Mom, what's an abortion?"—you might be able to say that an abortion is getting rid of the fetus of an unborn child. But then if your son or daughter says, "Mom, how do they do it?"—you may not know. The same might be true of contraceptive methods, venereal diseases, and so on.

A Christian couple may have a rather blasé attitude toward sex. For them, all the sexual questions have been answered. They have a rather satisfying sex life in their marriage, so they feel no real need to learn about contraception, venereal disease, the ethics of abortion, and so on. When a child asks them a question about sex, they are not prepared. That in itself can erect a barrier of communication. The child thinks, "It's no use to ask Mom and Dad, 'cause they don't know!" It is possible to prepare in advance of the big question.

This sort of thing happened to us. Our daughter asked us where babies come from when she entered the fourth grade. We weren't ready that particular day. We wanted to give her more than a simple, verbal explanation; we felt we needed some illustrations to show her what we were talking about. So my wife Beth said, "Honey, we want you to know this. We think it's important for you to know it now. But we need to get a book that will help us explain it to you. Would it be all right if we waited till next week?"

Of course, that was all right.

This didn't make Liesl feel that she'd asked something wrong. It didn't make her feel as though she'd been put down or put off. Yet her mom didn't rush into the teaching ill-prepared, either.

Beth went to our public library and selected a fairly explicit book about sexual intercourse and pregnancy. She brought it home, and she and Liesl spent some time reading it together. When Beth came downstairs from their session, I asked, "What did she have to say?"

Beth smiled. "After I'd explained it, she just said, 'Oh, yuck!'"

Liesl had gotten enough information to satisfy her curiosity, and sex held no further interest for her at the time.

I believe that it is possible to dump a lot more sex information on elementary school children than they are emotionally ready for or want. We can't expect most fourth graders to grasp the significance of the sex act. So why should we try to explain it to them? Parents and teachers should be aware of young peoples' needs and interests regarding sex. We should be ready to provide the "facts of life" at the appropriate time. And Christian parents should be ready to explain the moral standards that come with the gift of *sex*.

God meant a person's sexuality to be a great joy and blessing in life. And it will be when a young person knows how to use his sexual nature in a way that honors the Lord.

Values Clarification

Values clarification is part of a whole field of study known as *moral education*—studies which help a student shape his moral and ethical values for life. American public schools have always been engaged in moral education, in some form or another.

The colonial schools were church-sponsored schools, so they devoted a large share of each day's class time to moral education. They studied the Ten Commandments, the Sermon on the Mount, and the Bible's other ethical teachings.

When Horace Mann began the push for government-sponsored schools in the early 1800s, he stressed that educators should give students a moral education as well as an academic education. Even in the twentieth century, our public schools have given youth a moral education—though usually in a very subtle form. Consider the Pledge of Allegiance, which most elementary school students recite every morning:

I pledge allegiance to the flag of the United States of American, and to the Republic for which it stands—one nation under God, indivisible, with liberty and justice for all.

Simple, isn't it? Yet packed with moral and ethical teaching. It teaches young people that they should give their *allegiance*—their unswerving loyalty—to our nation. It teaches them that our nation lives and works "under God," rather like Paul's declaration to the philosophers of Athens, when he said, "In him (i.e., God) we live and move and have our being" (Acts 17:28). It teaches our youth that the nation offers "liberty and justice for all"; this nation was founded upon these ethical standards. The Pledge of Allegiance is a very subtle lesson in moral education . . . but a powerful one!

We could note several other forms of moral education. My point is, the schools *do* teach our young people moral and ethical standards. And values clarification is just one facet of that moral education.

Values clarification became popular in our public schools in the late 1960s and early 1970s. Various groups, Christian and non-Christian, attacked values clarification so ferociously that many schools abandoned it. Your school may still have values clarification, though, so you ought to know what it's about.

During my graduate studies, I received an intense indoctrination in values clarification. My professors felt it was "the coming thing," and they recommended that I use it in my classes quite liberally. The basic approach was this:

The teacher presents a hypothetical life situation to students, a situation that requires them to make a moral decision. Then the teacher asks a student to tell what he would do, and the class critiques that decision. Why did he take that course of action? What standard did he use to make that choice? Was his moral standard a valid one? Should he evaluate his standard? And, if so, how should he arrive at a new standard for making moral decisions? Here's one of the situations that a teacher might present to her class in a values clarification exercise:

In Europe, a woman was near death from a very bad disease, a special kind of cancer. There was one drug that the doctors thought might save her. It was a form of radium that a druggist was charging ten times what the drug cost him to make. He paid $200 for the radium and charged $2,000 for a small dose of the drug. The sick woman's husband, Heinz, went to everyone he knew to borrow the money, but he could only get together about $1,000, which was half of the cost. He told the druggist that his wife was dying, and asked him to sell it cheaper or let him pay later. But the druggist said, "No! I discovered the drug and I'm going to make money from it." So Heinz got desperate and broke into the man's store to steal the drug for his wife.

Should the man have done that? Why?[12]

This exercise is called a *simulation*. It's supposed to be a low risk way of allowing a student to make a difficult moral decision, before he must confront a similar decision in real life. When a student makes a choice about this problem in class, of course, he comes under attack from his fellow students and from the teacher. It would be a friendly, good-natured attack. A challenge to re-think what he decided to do. Nevertheless, the argument can be morally disconcerting, especially when the teacher or other students have more brilliant logic than the student under attack. They can find "good reasons" to condemn the choice he made, though the student knows he made them in keeping with a well-established moral standard (Christian or otherwise).

Often the class will bait a timid student, to see whether he would stand by his decision. A person of rather strong will and character will withstand their baiting—but young students might not. I can never recall a values clarification class where a *vicious* attack was made on a student's decision; it was always done in good humor. Nevertheless, the class tries to chip away at the student's position. Some students' attitudes are changed because they can't stand the criticism.

Here's a values-clarification exercise that a professor gave us in a graduate course. He said, "List twenty things that you like to do." (That was hard in itself. Try thinking of twenty things *you* like to do!) Then he said, "Beside each one, put the date you last did it. Note the ones that require advance preparation."

That little exercise taught me some interesting things about my own values. For one thing, I learned that I don't like doing things that require a lot of advance preparation! I noted that I like to go fly-fishing; in fact, that was near the top of my list. But I examined that. When was the last time I'd gone fly-fishing? Eleven months before, in Minnesota. And even though I liked to do it, I wasn't going to fly-fish again till we went to Minnesota again! Suddenly I discovered that I didn't really like to fly-fish. It was simply my excuse to get away from the telephone and the paperwork, to live in the woods for a week! If people asked me why I liked to go to Minnesota, I'd feel silly saying, "Because I like to sit under a tree in the woods." It seemed easier to say, "'Cause I like to go fly-fishing."

To this point, the exercise had helped me discover my own values without challenging me to defend them or abandon them. But the exercise continued. The professor said, "Check the things you like to do that your father liked to do." (Or, if you were a woman, the things your mother liked to do.) This made us question our values from a different angle. Should we repudiate some things we liked to do, simply because our parents liked them? Should we abandon some of our values to show our independence from Mom and Dad?

Educators usually claim that values clarification is morally neutral. But is it? A teacher using values clarification must assume that:

—there are no moral absolutes.

—all values are subjective.

—all values are acceptable.

So if a student in a values clarification class believes that certain things are absolutely wrong, he'll be challenged. He'll have to consider a wide variety of moral options. And he's supposed to conclude that *any* of those options could be right.

Another problem with values clarification is its potential for invasion of privacy. How can a teacher lead a class in values clarification unless the students disclose their personal values, attitudes, and habits? For example, the teacher might say, "Tell us what your Mom and Dad taught you about sex. Do you agree with what they said? What do you think about premarital sex, etc.?"

Some English teachers have their students keep a daily journal for a couple of weeks or so, to give them experience in creative writing. The students record what's happening in their lives each day: it's something they can write without doing any research. It may or may not be totally innocent. Yet a student may record some rather intimate things in the journal. So when the assignment is turned in, the teacher will discover much personal information about each student's life. What the teacher does from that point with that information is the main concern. The information must not become a topic of conversation in the teachers' lounge; nor should any child become a target of manipulation because of a set of beliefs with which a teacher does not agree.

(Realize that I am speaking of the possible abuses. When my own children have been participants in this activity, it was administered in the most innocent manner.)

Another problem with values clarification classes is that they use stories and situations that are strongly biased against most things that Christians would consider to be moral. They employ situations where it is difficult to make a choice that's true to the Lord—even situations where you *can't* make a choice that's true to the Lord, without violating some standard He has given us.

Remember the simulation of the woman with cancer and her distraught husband, Heinz? When that's presented to the class, the students must choose from these options: (1) let your wife die without the medicine, (2) get the medicine by breaking into the store, or (3) steal the money to buy it. The first option violates God's Word because it makes Heinz a party to murder. The second and third options violate God's Word because they make Heinz a thief. Yet these are the only choices the student is allowed. Here's another example: Your husband or wife is a very attractive person. Your best friend is very attracted to him or her. How would you want them to behave?

—Maintain a clandestine relationship so you wouldn't know about it.
—Be honest and accept the reality of the relationship.
—Proceed with a divorce.[13]

This is fairly typical of values clarification games. They present the student with a rotten situation, give him several rotten alternatives, then require him to take one of those alternatives and defend it. Frankly, not many of us will face such horribly difficult decisions. And if we do, God gives us other alternatives beside the ones presented in these classroom games. Any number of other possibilities are there, when we see the situation through Christian eyes. But these simulation games give the student only secular alternatives (Remember the separation of church and state?). So the only way a Christian student can "make the grade" is to take one of those secular alternatives—with no regard for God's alternatives—and figure out some way to defend it.

Here's another example of a simulation game that puts a Christian student in a no-win situation (I'm paraphrasing this from the story, "Alligator River."):

A young lady named Hester is in love with a young man who's gone across the river to build a cabin for them. He's been gone for some time, and Hester longs to see him. But a flood has taken out the bridge. So Hester goes to a young man she knows, named Ivan, who has a boat. She asks Ivan to take her across the river to see her fiance. Ivan says he certainly will, but the price is very high—she must compromise her virtue with him.

Hester is a good person. She declines the offer and goes to a local merchant, who also has a boat. But he does not want to get involved. So in desperation she goes back to Ivan and sells herself to him for a trip across the river.

Ivan fulfills his end of the bargain. He takes her across the river and, to be sure she's okay, he stays with her till she finds her sweetheart. Hester is then overcome with guilt and confesses her sin to her fiance. He grabs Ivan and thrashes him within an inch of his life, then turns to Hester and says he never wants to see her again. He doesn't care for her.

"Now," the teacher asks, "which of those people do you like the best? Which do you like the least?" (Aren't they all jewels?)

This game forces the student to condone—and defend—the actions of someone who's acted in a very ungodly manner. And this is fairly typical of values-clarification games. Richard A. Baer Jr., notes this in a perceptive article for a *secular* educators' journal, when he says:

... Biblical religion regards the love of God and the service of one's fellow human beings as the highest goals of man. But values clarification's emphasis on self-fulfillment and action on the basis of one's own desires and preferences stands in direct conflict with this religious value.[14]

I think this should raise a warning signal to any Christian parent. We need to check out any public-school program that uses simulations that force our youth to make choices that contradict the Christian values we have taught them.

You may have a hard time spotting the values clarification course, however, because it may be offered under a title other than "Values Clarification." One of the leading proponents of values clarification, Dr. Sidney Simon, has said, "I always bootlegged the values stuff under other titles. I was assigned to teach social studies in the elementary school and I taught values clarification. I was assigned Current Trends in American Education and I taught my trend."[15] In other words, Dr. Simon intended to change his students' values. He had an intentional "hidden curriculum," and he put it across in a very subtle way. The same thing may be happening in your public-school program. It may even be happening without the teacher realizing what she's doing to her students' values.

Values clarification will stir up a hot discussion in any teachers' meeting, or any parents' meeting! And with good reason: it affects the very root of our young people's standards for living. Someone once said that two topics are sure to start an argument—religion and politics. Well, values clarification is both. And we can't seem to reach an agreement on how it should be handled.

Certain social values should be taught to our young people for the common good of our community. This might come under the heading of "Civics," "Citizenship," or whatever. But what values should be taught? Under what label should they be taught? And who will do the teaching? There we disagree.

As I said, many school systems have banned values clarification from their curricula because it's such a "hot potato." But it may still continue in subtle and unrecognized forms. The computer classes now popular in our junior and senior high schools often use values clarification programs. They're not called values clarification, of course. But they may use some of the same concepts.

For instance, I recently attended a computer workshop that was tackling this problem: Suppose you were a truck driver who had to deliver a load of fruit from California to New York in so many days. You could take the northern route. There the weather is cool and your load is not likely to spoil; but you might run into snow and ice. You could take the southern route. There the weather is good for travel; but the heat might spoil your fruit. Or you could take the middle route. There the road conditions are rather good and the weather is reasonably good for your load; but you'll hit a lot of speed traps along the way. I chose the middle route. And hoping to beat my classmates, I broke the speed limit several times—and was arrested. I got to New York on time, but my speeding fines ate up all my profits. The bank repossessed my trucking rig.

That sort of game is a lot of fun, isn't it? But did you notice the moral decision I made? I broke the law to try to win the game. In a very low-key sort of way, the game called for me to clarify my values; and I chose to make a profit instead of obeying the law.

Because it's so hard to identify values clarification in your school's curriculum, you can best counteract its influence by teaching your children appropriate Christian values at home. Show them that they *do* have other alternatives, besides the secular alternatives. Help them decide how they would handle real moral choices in a way that honors the Lord. Look for those "teachable moments," when your son or daughter is ready to learn about values. Deuteronomy 6:7-10 says God expected the Jews to teach His law all through the day, in the simple events of home life. And we can do the same as Christians.

A moment of crisis can be a "teachable moment" for your child—when the family pet dies, when your daughter doesn't make the team, when your son has embarrassed himself in front of his friends. These can be good times for a heart-to-heart talk about the things we value as Christians.

Family outings give you good "teachable moments." When you're riding in the car, walking in the woods, watching a sports event, be ready to point out appropriate lessons in Christian standards. Without being preachy, you can give your children good guidance at such times.

Let's face it! Our children will get moral education in the public schools. They always have and they always will. So we Christian parents should give them the right kind of moral education at home. Let's teach them the standards a Christian should have in light of God's Word. Then our youth will be better prepared to "give an answer" when their teacher or classmates ask why they have those standards. (See 1 Peter 3:15, 16.)

NOTES

[1]Walter T. Brown, Jr., "Arkansas: So What?" *Moody Monthly*, May 1982, p. 15.

[2]Homer Duncan, *Humanism in Light of the Holy Scripture* (Lubbock, TX: Missionary Crusader, 1981), p. 83 ff.

[3]James H. Jauncey, *Science Returns to God* (Grand Rapids, MI: Zondervan, 1971), p. 20 ff.

[4]Opal Moore, *Why Johnny Can't Learn* (Milford, MI: Mott Media, 1975), p. 55 ff.

[5]*Ibid.*, p. 56.

[6]Martin Mawyer, "Arkansas: Where Creationism Lost Its Shirt," *Moody Monthly*, May 1982, p. 10 ff.

[7]Peggy Brick, "Sex Education Belongs in School," *Educational Leadership*, February 1981, p. 390.

[8]*Ibid.*, p. 394.

[9]Opal Moore, *op. cit.*, p. 107.

[10]Christian S. White IV, "Ineffectiveness of Sex Ed Shown by Simple Statistics," *About Issues*, July 1982, p. 21.

[11]"Newsfronts," *Education USA*, May 31, 1982, p. 318.

[12]Clive M. Beck, Brian S. Crittenden, and Edmund V. Sullivan, eds., *Moral Education: Interdisciplinary Approaches* (Toronto: University of Toronto Press, 1971), p. 33.

[13]Richard A. Baer, Jr., "Teaching Values in the Schools: Clarification or Indoctrination?" *Principal*, January 1982, p. 36.

[14]*Ibid.*

[15]Barbara M. Morris, *Change Agents in the Schools* (Ellicott City, MD: The Barbara M. Morris Report, 1979), p. 61.

Schoolbook Censorship

French Lick IN—Arthur Miller's "Death of a Salesman" has been banned from an English class at Springs Valley Community High School because the drama contains the words, "God damn!"

Baileyville ME—*Three Hundred Sixty-Five Days*, a graphic report written by Ronald J. Glasser, a physician who worked for a year in Vietnam, has been removed from the shelves of the Baileyville High School library because of the allegedly excessive use of four-letter words and their supposedly harmful influence on students.

Glenrose CA—Students need parental permission to see the school library's copy of *MS.* magazine.

Washington PA—Pressures have been exerted by parents to remove *The Adventures of Huckleberry Finn* from the shelves of Bucks County School District libraries because of racial tension (Mark) Twain's novel is alleged to create.[1]

All of these news stories came across the press wire in 1981. And all of them deal with schoolbook censorship.

What do you think of when you hear the word *censorship?* Book burnings? True, there have been public book burnings in America; but censorship does not always involve such radical measures as that. Censorship may be practiced by public pressure groups; but it may also be practiced by teachers, school administrators, librarians, educational agencies, state legislatures—even by book publishers themselves!

What is censorship? It is simply someone's conscious choice to use certain items of printed matter, to the exclusion of others. In other words, *censorship* is choosing what you (or other people) will and will not read.

If you accept this definition, you immediately realize that we have always practiced censorship in the public schools. And we always will. But there is a great deal of debate about the issue today, because many parents feel that censorship infringes on their children's rights and the way they want to train their children.

Thirty or forty years ago, school personnel tended to choose reading material that reflected traditional Judeo-Christian standards. But as our society has become more pluralistic, they have tried to present a wider variety of printed material to our students. And this has led to more conflict with parents who uphold the traditional Judeo-Christian values.

Many parents hope to shelter their children from rapid change. They say, "Oh, I'd like to move to the country so my kids would be in a small rural school, where there are no drugs or violence or other problems like that." But society's problems spread rapidly. Our children will be exposed to the hard facts of life in any school corporation, public or private. We are no longer isolated from the rest of the world. The mass media convey new ideas and life-styles from one country to another—even from one part of the same country to another part—faster than ever before. What starts as "the latest thing" in California will soon be "the latest thing" in the Midwest. And when the school staff chooses the books they will use, they must not only consider the Judeo-Christian ethic, they must consider all of the other life-styles and standards that are current in our society. Their job is tougher than ever!

Yet many influential people want stiffer censorship of the books that go into our public schools. The evangelist Jerry Falwell told a rally in Washington, D.C., in April 1979, that most public school textbooks are nothing more than "Soviet propaganda."[2] He told the crowd of 15,000 that "in school textbooks, pornography, obscenity, vulgarity and profanity are destroying our children's moral values." This rally thrust many evangelical Christian leaders into the eye of the censorship storm.

Mel and Norma Gabler of Longview, Texas have founded an organization known as Educational Research Analysts. They screen schoolbooks and recommend which ones local parent groups should try to ban. The Gablers began by opposing some of the textbooks used in the Texas schools; they focused their opposition at textbook publishers and their state textbook adoption committee. But the Gablers' well-publicized work prompted the formation of dozens of local pressure groups, bent on removing books from the public schools.

Conservative Christians and liberal humanists are constantly wrangling over the issue of schoolbook censorship. Both sides claim that the "Founding Fathers" held their particular philosophy. Both sides claim to be tolerant and say that their opposition is intolerant. Both sides claim to be in the majority. Both sides say that the other side wants to "take over the schools." Both sides blame the other for epidemic pregnancies and venereal disease. Both sides claim that the media is controlled by the other side. Both sides say, "We must stop them at all costs. Otherwise, our society is headed for disaster." And both sides use schoolbook censorship as a *cause celebre* to make their point.

Conservative Christians are not the only people trying to censor schoolbooks, however. Others want to remove other books that inflame their own feelings.

Activists such as Betty Friedan want the schools to ban books that discriminate against women. The Gay Liberation Movement wants to ban books that present homosexuality as a deviant practice. The National Association for the Advancement of Colored People (NAACP), the Congress on Racial Equality (CORE), the Southern Christian Leadership Conference (SCLC), and other civil-rights organizations want to ban books that portray black people in an unfavorable light. And the list goes on.

Several educators' organizations joined forces in 1979 to combat this push for more censorship. The American Association of School Administrators, the American Federation of Teachers, the National Council for the Social Studies, the National Council of Teachers of English, the National Education Association, and the Speech Communication Association were among the teachers' groups that linked arms to face the censorship battle. They were joined by the American Library Association, the International Reading Association, and other groups involving people outside the schools. Look over these names, and I think you will realize why each group would want to combat censorship. Each of them feels they need complete freedom to choose schoolbooks, in order to do their work properly.

What Gets Banned—and Why

If you were to read a list of all the books that might be banned from your school's library shelves this year, you might be surprised at the wide variety of things that are being removed. Here's a sample list of books that various schools have banned, along with the reason why:

Book	Reason for Banning
Go Ask Alice, by Anonymous	Profanity; sexual promiscuity
Soul on Ice, by Eldridge Cleaver	Profanity; incites to violence
Slaughterhouse Five, by Kurt Vonnegut	Profanity; sexual promiscuity
The Naked Ape, by Desmond Morris	Anti-creation; describes man as a higher animal
The Scarlet Letter, by Nathaniel Hawthorne	Adultery; depicts Christians in bad light
Huckleberry Finn, by Mark Twain	Racism
Future Shock, by Alvin Toffler	Condones sexual promiscuity and deviant life-styles
The Lord of the Flies, by William Golding	Racism; incites to violence
The Catcher in the Rye, by J.D. Salinger	Profanity; sexual promiscuity
1984 by George Orwell	Incites to violence
The Grapes of Wrath by John Steinbeck	Profanity; sexual promiscuity
Black Like Me, by John H. Griffin	Racism; incites to violence
Hawaii, by James Michener	Sexual promiscuity

National Geographic magazine	Nudity
Red Riding Hood, by Anonymous	Violence
Hansel & Gretel, by the Grimm Brothers	Violence

There is no distinct pattern to what is being pulled from our school's library shelves. Anything might be challenged. In fact, the Bible has been challenged in some school districts because Jewish constituents feel the New Testament is anti-Semitic, feminists feel Paul is chauvinistic, pacifists feel the Old Testament condones war, and so on. In fact, if school personnel pulled off the shelves any book that might offend some of their constituents, the shelves would be empty! Our society is so diverse—we have so many conflicting opinions and life-styles—that every book is apt to offend some of us.

But let's think about the criteria that evangelical Christian parents would like to see school officials use in selecting books for our children.

We live in an era that extols realism and relevance. This is true in books, films, drama, the fine arts, and even the TV docu-dramas. Most people want writers to "tell it like it is." This cry is often used to justify profanity, promiscuity, and violence in schoolbooks. These things are supposed to make books "more realistic" or "more true to life."

I have heard liberal-thinking parents say, "What's wrong with having profanity in school library books? Don't you think your children have already heard those words? Don't you think they can understand what the writer is trying to say?" The answer is "yes," of course. But I don't want my children to feel those words are acceptable to use. When my school buys that type of literature, it is, in effect, placing the community's stamp of approval upon it. And I object to that.

My liberal friends respond, "Don't you feel it's appropriate for your children to be exposed to the rough side of life? After all, you can't shelter them all their lives. They can't live in the Christian milieu forever."

When my children attend a public school, I know they are not living in a sheltered environment. In any high school, if they want to learn the latest "street language," all they have to do is go to the restroom and read the graffiti on the walls. (When I became vice-principal of a high school a few years ago, my predecessor remained on staff as the athletic director. A few days after the change, he came into my office and said, "Well, the kids know who the new vice-principal is. They quit writing my name on the restroom walls and put yours there.") We can't control what kids say in hallways or write on the restroom walls; so I know my children will be exposed to the seamy side of life. But I don't believe we should teach "restroom literature" in the classroom or recommend it to students who visit the school library.

The Bible says, As a man "thinketh in his heart, so is he" (Proverbs 23:7). So it exhorts us, "Whatsoever things are true, whatsoever things are honest, whatsoever things are just, whatsoever things are pure, whatsoever things are lovely, whatsoever things are of good report; if there be any virtue, and if there be any praise, think on these things" (Philippians 4:8). The thoughts we have will shape the kind of people we become. The Christian parent should remember this when considering the books his children read.

If what we read affects our thoughts, and if our thoughts affect our behavior, doesn't it logically follow that reading profane or violent material will affect our behavior, too? Even a passing exposure to pornography, profanity, or violence—to anything that cheapens the value of human life—is bound to affect the mind of the reader, either consciously or unconsciously. And eventually it will affect that person's conduct.

Some parents will read this and say, "Come on, now. Surely these things aren't in our school library books and textbooks, are they? Profanity? Promiscuity? Bloody violence? Aren't you exaggerating things a bit?"

No, I'm not. Granted, you may not find these things in the books your elementary school children are bringing home. But the farther you go in the educational process, the more of these things you will encounter in school library books and textbooks. The things I've mentioned are often found in junior high and senior high books, because educators assume that these older pupils can deal with such things on "an adult level." Yet I believe most evangelical parents would object to these things.

Along this line, let me add that any Christian parent who wants to censor his children's schoolbooks and magazines, but allows them relatively free and unrestricted TV viewing, is being inconsistent. My experience convinces me that TV offers more alcoholism, sex, violence, and bad language in nightly doses than our students will ever receive from their schoolbooks. Nearly every sports program that teenagers want to watch, for example, is sponsored by a major beer brewery. Beer is being hawked and promoted by some outstanding athletes that the kids admire. What a powerful influence that must have on our young people night after night! So before you condemn your school officials for what they allow your kids to read, check what you allow them to see at home. Why complain about what they absorb for thirty minutes a day from one of their schoolbooks when you allow them to watch worse things for three hours a night on television?

A friend of mine was watching a TV program about a couple of homosexual young women. His daughter, who was just entering third grade, was watching the program with him. He assumed his eight year old didn't understand the situation. But about fifteen minutes into the show, she gave him a puzzled look and said, "Daddy, I don't know what's going on here unless those two gals are lesbians."

Obviously, his little girl had not been sheltered from the facts of life! Yet as she continues to watch TV, her father ought to continue watching with her; he ought to read schoolbooks with her; and he ought to discuss those crude "realities" with her in a Christian light. This does not mean that he should "have school" with her, but that he should be sensitive to the "teachable moment."

Methods of Censorship

Censorship methods fall into two basic categories: methods that are acceptable to a *majority* of the people in a given school community, and methods that are acceptable to a *minority*. Obviously, school personnel want to censor books in a way that the majority of their constituents will accept. Most people in a community are willing to accept schoolbook censorship when . . .

. . . a mother takes her children to the public library and chooses certain books for them to read.

. . . a teacher chooses to use certain books for her pupils, because she feels those books will expedite the teaching process.

. . . a textbook adoption committee chooses one publisher's textbook series (and in so doing rejects five others).

These methods of censorship are so common and widely accepted that most parents probably don't even consider them censorship. But when we choose to give one book to a child to read, we automatically choose *not* to give other books to him. We are being censors whether we realize it or not! And most folks would accept these voluntary methods of censorship.

When I was a choir director, I often purchased current hit songs that the students liked for our spring pops concert. One year I bought a song that contained the words "turns me on." All of us knew it meant a sexual turn on, of course. We discussed it briefly and agreed that the line should be changed. One of the students volunteered to come back the next day with some alternative lines. In fact, she returned with several alternatives for that line—alternatives that fit the poetry, fit the mood, and flowed right in with the song. The choir members were happy with the line we finally picked.

That was censorship, wasn't it? Yet it was the kind of censorship most people will accept, because it was purely voluntary. School officials can encourage this sort of censorship, and we parents can encourage our students to do it themselves.

When I was vice-principal of another high school, the choir director chose to do a number from "Jesus Christ Superstar" for his spring concert. It was "I Don't Know How to Love Him," the love song that Mary Magdalene sings for Jesus. While it's a beautiful song from the secular standpoint, it does suggest a sexual relationship between Mary and Jesus.

One Christian girl in the choir felt very uncomfortable about singing it, and she handled the problem in a way that I think was very appropriate. She didn't circulate a petition; she didn't appear before the school board; she didn't park herself in the principal's office to lodge a protest. She simply went to the choir director and said, "As a Christian, I object to the message of this song, and I don't think I ought to sing it. May I have permission to stand in place and not sing that number?"

The director said, "Certainly!"

This girl did not make a big scene out of her objection. She didn't climb down off the risers and walk offstage. She simply stood there in her place and did not sing that song. She was true to her convictions. She shared her Christian testimony with the choir director (where it counted the most in this situation). But she was not abusive or judgmental in what she said or did. She practiced good self-censorship, and her peers accepted it.

We all practice self-censorship, whether we realize it or not. No one objects to that. But most people would object to censorship when ...

... a parent marches into the school and demands that a particular book be removed from the textbook list or the library shelves.

... a principal orders that a certain book be removed from the school, because he or she objects to its contents.

... a school board bans a certain book from all of its schools, because they object to its contents.

People object to these methods of censorship because they impose the views of one person (or one group) upon everyone else. The censor may have broad enough support in the community to "get away with it"; but, more likely, he will be opposed. He may be taken to court in a losing case, particularly if the school has no written review procedure for printed material.

The Island Trees Decision

On July 25, 1982, the United States Supreme Court handed down a key decision in this regard. The case involved the Island Trees Union Free School District of Nassau County, New York. A group of students there had brought suit against the school board for removing three novels from their school libraries. The students said the school board had violated their constitutional rights. Here's how the Associated Press reported it:

Washington, D.C.—The Supreme Court, condemning arbitrary book-banning by school boards as a violation of free speech, ruled 5-4 today parents and students can sue to challenge the removal of books from school libraries.

In a sharply worded decision, Justice William Brennan declared, "Local school boards may not remove books from school library shelves simply because they dislike the ideas contained in those books and seek by their removal to prescribe what shall be orthodox in politics, nationalism, religion or other matters of opinion."[3]

In the Island Trees decision, the Supreme Court ruled no school board can determine what ideas are standard for their community, and they cannot censor schoolbooks to reflect those standards. When one group (in this case, the school board) tries to impose its reading values upon the entire school system, there is a likelihood that other community groups will recoil with a vengeance. So will the courts.

Yet censorship is a fact of life. We practice censorship every time we purchase a school textbook or library book. So censorship will not go away. The only question is, "What sort of censorship will the public accept?" It's quite evident that Christians wouldn't accept arbitrary, bureaucratic censorship, nor will others accept it from them. All people will insist on having a voice in these decisions.

Some Guidelines

Conflicts such as the one at Island Trees will often arise because the school system does not have adequate procedures for dealing with censorship. Here are some guidelines that many schools have found to be helpful. You might want to recommend these to your principal and/or your school board. They could prevent serious problems in the future:

1. *The school board should have a clear procedure for*

choosing instructional materials. Whether books or audiovisuals or whatever, the material they purchase should be selected in a prescribed way. Parents, teachers, and principals should know the school board's policy for selecting materials; it should not be done arbitrarily.

For example, let us say the school board has a policy of allowing each school librarian a certain budget for each year. Suppose the board directs the librarian to purchase new books that the teachers of that school have requested (using written request forms). If some parent complains about a library book, the librarian has a written record that the books was specifically requested by a teacher. The librarian also has the standing approval of the school board to make the purchase she made. Some schools form their own book selection committees comprised of parents, teachers, a couple of students, and the librarian.

But if the librarian purchased whatever books she liked, how could the school board respond to a complaint? Librarians who receive little or no input from other teachers, students, and parents seem to be in a position of personal vulnerability that is unnecessary.

The mother of a fifth-grade girl recently became upset when her daughter started checking out library books by Judy Blume. (This writer has won many awards, but she has also aroused considerable criticism because her books contain "street language" and "realistic" racial prejudice.) So the mother went to her pastor and said, "What should I do? I can tell my daughter not to bring these books home. But as a parent, I'm concerned that they are on the open library shelves, available to any child who wants them. I believe they are degrading."

The minister suggested that she talk with the school principal. So she did. She brought some of the books to the principal's office and shared the contents that were particularly upsetting to her. The principal was surprised to find this in the school's library books. She said, "Why don't you go and talk with the librarian? To be honest, I don't select the library books; the librarian does. So you need to ask her why she made these selections."

The mother gathered up the stack of books and walked down the hall to the library. By now the children had gone home, so they could talk very openly with one another.

"Mrs. X, you're being very unreasonable," the librarian said. "Judy Blume has won many children's book awards. Her books have been endorsed by educators and publishers from coast to coast. They are some of the best literature for children today, even though you may disagree with what she has to say. So we're going to keep these books on the shelves."

Needless to say, this mother was very dissatisfied. She had taken a proper step by going to her principal. But if her school district had had a formal review procedure, that confrontation between her and the librarian would not have occurred. She would have been able to file a formal request for the books to be reviewed, without anyone denouncing her as an "unreasonable" person. This leads me to the second point.

2. *The school board should have a written procedure for dealing with complaints.* For example, every school should have a printed form that anyone can fill out, in order to lodge a complaint about a schoolbook. This form should ask questions such as:

— What is the book's author, title, publisher, and date of publication?

— How was the book brought to your attention? (If you say, "My child brought it home one day," your school officials get a much different impression than if you say, "I heard about it at a rally of one hundred fifty parents at the V.F.W. Hall last night.")

— Do you represent yourself or a group of people?

— Have you read the entire book? (Your answer had

better be "Yes!" *Never* read a couple of passages from a book your child brings home, and then storm into the principal's office to complain.)

—What do you approve of in the book? (Cite specific pages and paragraphs that show what you feel is helpful in the book.)

—What do you disapprove of in the book? (Again, cite specific examples.)

—Can you recommend another book that would convey as valuable a perspective on the same issue?

—What is your name, address, and telephone number?

Most schools will not ask you to meet with the committee that reviews your complaint; that's the purpose of the form. You are not allowed to argue, cajole, and "sell" the committee on your ideas. You have submitted your criticism on the standard form, and they will review the book in light of your criticism. You may win or lose your case.

The written procedure should specify how the school board will set up the committee to review a book complaint; this also should not be arbitrary. The committee should include parents, nonparent citizens from the community, and school personnel. The board may also want to draw up some guidelines for this committee, telling them how to evaluate each complaint.

This written complaint procedure should guide the parents as well as the school officials in an orderly method of dealing with book challenges. School officials are obliged to consider *every* challenge; and in our diverse society, they are sure to come.

School officials may get defensive when the schoolbooks are challenged because they think parents are questioning their own integrity. (Sometimes parents do!) But if your school system has a clearly defined complaint procedure, it will tend to remove any personal vendetta from the discussion.

3. *The school should not place any restrictions on the*

material until this review has been completed. I know it would be easier to pull that book from the shelf and hide it in a desk drawer to avoid the hassle. But school officials should let the review process run its course. This usually will take only a few days.

When you challenge a schoolbook, you can expect your principal to have an informal meeting with you. He or she may try to determine why you object to the book, and will try to convince you that the book is all right. In some cases, you will change your mind. But if you still feel the book should be withdrawn from your school's library or the classroom, ask to file a written request for review. The committee cannot start until you have placed it in writing. But then procedures for dealing with your challenge will move rather swiftly.

You may expect your school to inform the local newspaper and other news media that a meeting of the committee will be held, soliciting other parents' opinions about the book before the meeting. When this happens, you may get tremendous public support for your challenge—or you may get tremendous resistance. But your challenge becomes a matter for the whole community to consider.

Why Stir Up Trouble?

I'm sure that many Christian parents who read these lines will wonder whether they should get involved in schoolbook censorship. Perhaps you feel the same way. Perhaps you think the public school system of America is a monolithic institution that takes its orders direct from Washington, so you can't have much effect on what your local school does. Perhaps you feel it's futile to object to any books that are offensive to you.

That's not so. The farthest-removed authority in choosing books for your school is your state's textbook adoption committee. And even when they make a decision about school textbooks, your hands are not tied.

You still have options for giving your child other books. (See the next chapter.)

In 1980, the Association for Supervision and Curriculum Development, the Association of American Publishers, and the American Library Association conducted a survey to determine how schoolbook challenges affect the overall process of book selection. The survey was conducted in all fifty states; there were 1,891 respondents. And here's what they found:

Nearly one-fifth of the local school administrators and one-third of the school librarians reported some challenge to classroom or library materials between 1978 and 1980. But the educators did not feel these challenges hindered their work. "As a check both on unavoidable human error and on the occasionally arbitrary exercise of authority, such challenges may be viewed as an essential element in the overall selection process," the report said.[4]

In exactly half of all incidents cited, the challenged material was altered, restricted, or removed prior to a formal review. In approximately 40 percent of all cases no one was assigned to reevaluate the material. About a third of the local challenges were overruled. But in 22 percent of all recent cases, the material questioned was ultimately removed from the school, and in approximately 30 percent some other action was taken limiting student access.[5]

Of course, the important thing is not how *often* schoolbooks are challenged, but how the challenge is handled. If a book challenge pits school officials against parents, it will have long-range detriment to the learning environment of your school. But, if a book challenge causes school officials and parents to work together and set common goals, it can forge a healthier school environment than you've ever had.

A schoolbook challenge may draw you into the textbook adoption process, which I will describe in more detail in Chapter 7. At this point, let me say that textbook adoption work might give you the opportunity to review books with an atheistic university professor, the wife of a prominent businessman, a retired schoolteacher, and a wide variety of others who have children in your school or who are involved in your community in some other significant way. Serving on such a textbook committee can open your eyes to the diverse needs of your community. While the committee may not always adopt the particular textbooks you want as an evangelical Christian, you can be a spiritual "leaven" in the process. That's an exciting opportunity.

Positive Censorship

As I said at the beginning of this chapter, censorship is not only the removing of certain books that you don't approve; it's choosing the books that you do. I think Christian parents need to practice more of this positive censorship for their children. We need to give our children some good alternatives to the books we do not want them to read.

For example, an adolescent girl may be preoccupied with romance. Most Christian bookstores in this country have a variety of romantic novels with Christian themes that would be most appropriate for your girl to read—books like *Christy,* by Catherine Marshall or the Grace Livingston Hill novels. Why not buy your daughter some of these books for her birthday, Christmas, or some other special occasion?

An adolescent boy often likes to read tales of adventure, and there are some excellent books in this vein. The Danny Orlis Series, The *Bradford Family Adventures* and *Eddie Series* from Standard, the *Code Name Sebastian* series, the Hardy Boys novels—you will find a variety at your bookstore. Gladys Hunt's book, *Honey for a Child's Heart,*[6] gives you a list of wholesome books for your child, regardless of his age or interest area. And I'm sure your Christian bookstore owner would be happy to recommend others.

As you buy books of this kind, you support writers who are trying to provide wholesome reading material for your son or daughter. And that's part of the long-range solution. We Christians are not being the "salt" we should be in the publishing world, because we are not buying and reading what quality Christian authors have produced. If we did, bookstores would stock more of their books. Christian authors would be asked to write more. And the current glut of profanity, promiscuity, and violence would abate.

Let's say you went to your physician with excess weight, diabetes, and high blood pressure. Your doctor would ask, "What have you been eating?"

"Well," you'd say, "for the past twenty-five years I've had pie, cake, or ice cream every night after supper. Potato chips while I watch TV. Coke and a peanut butter sandwich for breakfast. But I need to be cured of my health problems, Doc. Give me something that will cure me now."

Your doctor can't do that, of course. There is no quick remedy for a problem you have brought on yourself over a period of many years. So it is with the books we read. If we buy sex tabloids at the grocery store, off-color novels at the newsstand, and racy hardbacks on the best-seller list, we will get more of the same. But if we buy and read wholesome literature year after year, publishers will give us more. They are in the business of selling books.

As you get involved in the life of your school, you can help to bring changes for the better. But the changes will come only if you support your *public* stance with a *private* stance for what is wholesome and Christ-honoring. Anytime you choose something for you or your children to read, you practice censorship. Will it be Christian censorship or carnal censorship? You decide.

120

NOTES

[1]Robert P. Doyle. "Censorship and the Challenge to Intellectual Freedom," *The Principal,* January 1982, p. 8.

[2]Edward B. Jenkinson, "Protest Groups Exert Strong Impact," *Publishers' Weekly,* October 29, 1979, p. 42.

[3]"Court OKs Book Removal Lawsuits," *Fort Wayne News-Sentinel,* July 25, 1982, p. 1.

[4]Michelle Marder Kamki, "Censorship vs. Selection — Choosing Books for Schools," *American Education,* March 1982, pp. 11-15.

[5]*Ibid.,* p. 13.

[6]Gladys Hunt, *Honey for a Child's Heart* (Grand Rapids, MI: Zondervan Publishing House, 1978), pp. 125-182.

Choosing the Textbooks

The phone rings. It's Mary Smith, principal at your son's elementary school.

"Mr. Brown, the school board is getting ready to purchase a new set of math and science textbooks for our schools," she says. "They're organizing a Textbook Adoption Committee to review the books and make recommendations. Would you be willing to serve on this committee?"

Hundred of parents across America will receive such a phone call this year. That may surprise you. Yet in nearly every school district of this country, you can help to choose the textbooks your children will use in the public schools. You are most likely to be invited if you already know something about your district's textbook adoption process, and if you have a cordial relationship with your school officials.

In over twenty states[1], textbooks are chosen by state and local Textbook Adoption Committees. These states follow a general pattern:

Each year the State Textbook Adoption Committee will consider books for certain subject areas such as math and science, English composition and literature, vocational courses, or some other area. Publishers will submit their new books on that subject to the state committee, which compiles a list of recommended books for local Textbook Adoption Committees to consider. Then the local Textbook Adoption Committee selects the books that they feel should be used in their district. They submit their choices to the local school board, which in most cases will approve what the local committee has chosen. (That way, if there's any "flak" about a particular book, the elected school board members don't get blamed—their Textbook Adoption Committee does!)

You probably will not be asked to serve on a state Textbook Adoption Committee. These people are respected educators who are appointed by the state Commissioner of Education, the legislature, or some other state authority. (This is unfortunate, because several states require their local textbook committees to choose books from the state list; and if no parents are on the state committee, that committee may make some ill-advised choices. If your state has such a procedure, ask your state legislator to press for putting some noneducators on the state textbook committee.) Other states make available for adoption any publisher's text. In these states, the possibilities for some "one issue" text being chosen are fairly obvious. Local screening committees are of critical importance.

Local Textbook Committees are open to you. Most states with Local Textbook Committees *require* that some noneducators serve on these groups.[2] In other words, some parents and other taxpayers from the community must be appointed to the local textbook committee. This is a good place for you as a Christian parent to have effective input.

It is generally safe to assume that a school must involve local citizens in the planning, implementation, and evaluation of any federally-funded program if it has to do with the instruction of students. Even in states that don't invite parents to serve on Textbook Adoption Committees, you still can influence the choice of some of the school's materials. That's because Federal law requires a school board to allow parents and patrons to view any of the instructional materials used in a program underwritten with Chapter 1 funds.[3] About ninety percent of all public schools in the country have a Chapter 1 program. *Whenever federal funds are used to buy instructional materials, you have a right to come into your school office and review the materials.* Parents or other citizens rarely do this, possibly because they do not know they can.

Your state may also require the school board to set up a Parents Advisory Council to monitor materials purchased for any course that gets state tax support. States often underwrite a school's vocational courses, for example—agriculture, home economics, business, and so on—and the state may attach the "strings" of a local Parents Advisory Council to assist in the decision-making processes of these programs. If your state has such a policy, it's another opportunity for you to assist in the selection of instructional materials used in your school.

If you are a Christian parent who has an interest in the written curriculum of your school, if you can rationally examine textbooks and calmly discuss their merits, perhaps you should be serving on a Parents Advisory Council or Textbook Adoption Committee. You will represent not only yourself but other parents who have similar concerns.

How to Get Appointed

How do you go about getting on a local Textbook Adoption Committee? I wish I could answer that definitively. But the procedure varies from one state to another, even from one district to another. Often a school board will ask each principal to recommend one non-educator to serve on the textbook committee. The P.T.A. or a faculty group may appoint the textbook committee. Or the school board may simply wait for volunteers. But no matter who has the job of selecting the committee, and no matter how it's done, few people are willing to serve on a Textbook Adoption Committee. After all, it's hard work!

You can see how a good relationship with your school officials would help at this point. If some time in the past you have stormed into the school livid with rage about something that was being done, and acted like a flint-faced reformer, you probably will not be asked to serve on one of these committees! But if you have been a supportive parent who has been involved in the work of the school in some positive way, you have a better chance of being chosen.

You also have a better chance if you have some expertise in the subject being considered. For example, if you are a beautician or an auto mechanic, you may well be appointed to a Parents Advisory Council on vocational education. Or if your Textbook Adoption Committee is considering math or accounting books this year, and you happen to be an accountant, so much the better.

You may be chosen to represent a certain religious point of view. If you are a Roman Catholic, for example, and your community has a sizable Roman Catholic population, the school board may take care to include you on the textbook committee because you will act as a bellwether of Catholic interests. You could point out for example that your Catholic friends might object to using Irving Stone's novel, *The Agony and the Ecstasy,* because one of its chief characters is a corrupt Renaissance pope. Other committee members would not be aware of this.

I believe a Textbook Adoption Committee or Parents Advisory Council is most effective when it includes people from many ethnic, religious, and racial backgrounds. Of course, in a complex society such as ours, no textbook will completely satisfy everyone. But a carefully chosen textbook committee will reflect a wide enough variety of views that it will alert school officials to a potential backlash about a given book. Some areas of the country have such a broad cultural diversity that it will be hard to satisfy even a majority of the committee. But this makes the committee's work even more important. Here the people of your community can meet in a nonvolatile situation to discuss the hard issues of politics, morality, and even religion as they try to select curriculum materials for the public schools.

If you would like to serve on such a committee, begin by asking your principal whether your district has such committees and how people are chosen to serve on them. If your district does not have textbook committees, suggest to the school board that they organize one. If you live in a large urban school district, and your principal is not familiar with the textbook selection process, try calling the superintendent's office. Naturally, you have less chance of being selected for a textbook committee if you do live in a large and populous school district; but even large school districts need a broad diversity of members on their committees. Who knows? You may be just the type of person the school officials are looking for!

Committee Guidelines and Procedures

If you find yourself on a Textbook Adoption Committee or a Parents Advisory Council, you probably will be asked to examine books for a specific subject and/or grade level. In other words, you won't be reviewing all of the textbooks that come before the committee this year. You probably will be given a checklist of things to consider in your particular set of books. For example, in some communities it's important to see that reading texts include illustrations of Hispanics, blacks, white, and Asians. The guidelines may tell you to look for at least a few stories that show well-adjusted children living with a single parent. There may be dozens of such factors on your checklist. So if you're a factory worker who has just been appointed to a Textbook Adoption Committee, don't feel intimidated by the task. The school officials won't just hand you a stack of books and say, "Read these and let us know what you think." You will be given some guidance.

If the committee guidelines don't include a checklist of strong points and weaknesses, construct your own checklist, based on the guidelines. Consider every important aspect of the book.[4] Then rank the books according to your preference. Don't just tell the committee, "This book is great! All the rest are terrible." Know why you prefer certain books and rank them from first to last choice.

Make sure that you read every word of every book under consideration before you rank your choices. Don't just casually thumb through, looking at topics. If a committee member said, "I really object to these fifth-grade readers," my first question would be, "Have you read them all the way through?" And I would expect the person to say, "Yes!" Anyone who's expressing a very strong opinion about a textbook should know what he's talking about. He should not base his opinion on incomplete information, secondhand information, or conjecture.

Of course, graded textbooks are not the only teaching materials that we find in the classroom. Paperback books—often novels—may be used in junior high and senior high literature courses. Since these are considered "supplementary materials," they may not be brought to your committee; the individual teacher may choose them. However, common sense dictates that "supplementary materials" should also come under the scrutiny of your committee, because this material may be quite controversial. Ask to see any supplementary materials that may be used along with the textbooks you are considering. You might spare the teacher an unnecessary confrontation with other parents in your community.

Ask to review filmstrips, video tapes, and any other audiovisuals that the teacher would use along with a given textbook. Audiovisuals may also prove controversial, especially in subjects such as sex education or biology.

As you examine the textbooks, you may want to show them to other parents in the community and get their opinions. This way, when you return to your committee meeting, you are speaking not only for yourself but as a representative of your community. If a committee knows that others feel as you do about a particular book, your voice may be heeded.

Be tactful about doing this. If you feel that a large segment of the community would be upset by a certain book, don't dash out to solicit criticism. Go to the committee first. Express your own reservations about the book. Then ask how you might sound out other people's feelings. When the committee helps you make this decision, they won't feel threatened or defensive about your desire to contact other people. And by all means, raise this question early, well before the committee's final choices are due.

Take a hypothetical case:

Carl Sagan's popular book, *Cosmos,* is being considered as a supplementary text for a physical science course. You are a conservative evangelical Christian, a member of the textbook committee, and you object to

128

Dr. Sagan's book. When you are seated around the table with your committee, you might say something like this: "I would not want our committee to choose the book *Cosmos,* because it contradicts the Christian teaching I have given my children. I'm sure the same would be true of other Christian parents."

"Can you be specific?" someone will ask.

"Yes, I can. Dr. Sagan argues that earthly life was *not* created by God, but that it evolved from simple atoms and molecules. Other science books describe evolution and pass over the Bible's account of creation; but Dr. Sagan doesn't do that. He argues that divine creation is an old-fashioned idea that we don't need anymore.[5] He also says that the Christian faith grew out of pagan religions and ancient superstition, so it ought to be discarded.[6] As a Christian parent, I would oppose the purchase of this book. And I feel there may be many other people in this community who will be very angry if this book is chosen. I feel we should solicit the public's views in as broad a manner as possible over the next two or three weeks to see whether they feel as strongly as I think they do. How might we get their opinions?"

There are several ways, of course. You could simply show the book to your friends. You could display and discuss the book in church meetings, since you feel Christians would raise the most objections to the book. You could invite people to borrow a sample copy from the school board office and report their opinions. Let the committee decide which method is best. But do not solicit other people's opinions in any covert way. All of your dealings with the committee should be open and aboveboard.

Yes, it is valid for you to object to a textbook on religious grounds.[7] Most of the teachers in your school may live outside your community and have religious ideals that are significantly different from those of you and your neighbors. A book that offends you might not offend them. If so, alert them to a book that will clash strongly with your religious ideals. The teachers may engage you in a spirited debate about the book; but that's all right. What better time is there to thresh through the issue? The book has not yet been chosen. It's not in the classroom. No one has been alienated.

Look for trends and themes. Some of the trends in modern textbooks certainly should concern you as a Christian parent.

For example, many young people seem bent on self-destruction because the pressures of our society are too much for them. A sickness of mind and spirit overshadows many of today's youth. Unfortunately, school supplementary reading lists often deal with subjects that are depressing in themselves, and they deal with them in a way that offers no hope to youth. A student may be offered books about:

    —a teenager who has to choose between two parents.

    —a girl who lives with alcoholic parents and suffers all the problems associated with that.

    —a girl who has been raped by the son of a leading man in town, and who can get no justice because the father can "buy off" the local officials.

    —a teenager who wants to sue his parents for malpractice.

Supplementary reading lists often deal with "street themes," such as the story of a boy who gets addicted to alcohol and drugs and finally kills himself. By no means should we avoid dealing with "street themes." But many of these books leave the reader with a feeling of hopelessness and despair. They feed the problems instead of providing answers.

When I discuss this trend with other educators, one of them is sure to say, "Well, we have to provide realistic materials for our students." But I would not equate hopelessness with realism. I contend that we should choose textbooks that deal with real life problems in a manner that offers hope.

On the other hand, if we reject a book because we feel it is too negative, we must be sure to replace it with a book of quality. Christians may tend to be too saccharine in our tastes. We may want sweet, innocent little stories that have no instructive value and give a distorted Pollyanna view of the world. The world certainly isn't a Pollyanna place; we know that. But there is a wealth of quality books that deal with the problems of the world in a practical manner. These are the books we need. Education must prepare our children to live in a real world, and the reading material we give them should offer constructive answers to the problems they will face in the world.

As you evaluate textbooks and other instructional material, ask yourself, "Does this deal squarely with the issue at hand? Does it give the student a positive vision for the future? Does it show the student how to become a better person?" These questions will help you consider the true theme of the textbook material.

If You Are Outvoted ...

The educators probably will have a majority vote on your committee; most textbook committees are set up that way. So the group may decide to adopt a book, even though you and other local parents have raised strong objections to it. Now what can you do?

You might be tempted to do many different things at this point. You might fire off a letter to the editor of your local newspaper and air your grievance in public. You might turn into a human buzz saw, ripping up the reputations of the people who voted against you.

Or you might kindly express your convictions to the committee once again. This is far better. Tell why you feel the book is not appropriate for the students in your community, and point out that other parents feel as you do. Say, "I realize that I cannot force my beliefs on other people, of course. But I believe this particular book will cause conflict between our teachers and many parents in our community. I believe conflict makes good education more difficult. I care too much for our teachers, our children, and our school to stand by and let that happen. So I hope the committee will reconsider this decision."

Perhaps the committee *will* reconsider, when they see how earnest you are. But if they insist on buying the book, you have several options available: (1) You can request alternate reading material for that course. (2) You can discuss the textbook with the teacher who actually will be using it. (3) You can discuss the book with your child, pointing out why you disagree with it. Let's consider each of these options in more detail.

1. Alternative Reading Material. This is very easy to do in a literature class; if you object to a particular novel that's being read, ask the teacher to assign a different novel to your son or daughter. It's also easy to ask for alternate material in a social studies class. If you object to a supplementary text about a problem such as drug addiction or suicide, ask the teacher to assign a more constructive book on that subject to your child.

We have friends who were recently attempting to rear a boy who was not their own child. This boy had suffered indescribable emotional and physical abuse in his natural home. His junior high literature teacher assigned a novel for supplementary reading that contained a great amount of gore and terror. While these parents recognized that this boy needed to confront his past and work through the heartache he had experienced, they felt this particular choice of reading material would reawaken the trauma of his past in a negative and possibly harmful manner. Upon the request of the parents, the teacher assigned a different novel for that young man to read. (This year the teacher assigned the alternate novel to the entire class. He must have decided it was the better of the two books.)

Elementary schoolteachers may be more ready to assign alternative material, because they have been trained to give more individualized instruction. Secondary schoolteachers tend to be oriented toward large-group instruction, with everyone in the class studying the same thing. But I have noticed a shift toward more individualized instruction, accommodating each student's needs, even at the secondary level. Some teachers will deny your request for alternate material, but it won't hurt to ask.

Literature classes at the upper grade levels are often elective anyway. In that case, your son or daughter could simply choose not to take a course that's using an objectionable book.

Let's take that a step farther: Let's say that a high school literature class will be studying the play, "Inherit the Wind." This play concerns the famous John Scopes evolution trial in Dayton, Tennessee, and many fundamentalist Christians are offended by its anti-religious bias. If most people in your community are fundamentalist, then the majority of students might choose not to take the class, and the class simply would not materialize. (Of course, the Textbook Adoption Committee should have realized that the community was so strongly opposed to "Inherit the Wind," and have chosen another play. But as I said, textbook committees do make mistakes.)

2. Meeting With the Teacher. When you meet with the teacher who will use a particular textbook, you can gauge what sort of "hidden curriculum" he or she will have on that subject. The views of the teacher standing before the class are probably more important than the textbook itself. Some pupils won't read all of the textbook anyway; but all of them will hear the views of the teacher. And the teacher's "hidden curriculum" may come through loud and clear when a controversial topic surfaces in the classroom.

Suppose that you raised warning flags about a particular biology textbook that you felt would disturb many Christian parents in your community because it emphasizes evolution. Yet the textbook is adopted. You could ask to meet with the teacher of that course to make him aware of the problem you foresee. Most teachers will be grateful for this. It will cause them to be especially sensitive to the students' religious teaching, when they deal with that section of the book.

You may also find that the teacher's "hidden curriculum" will offset the bias of the book. I'm acquainted with two Christian high school biology teachers who could use *any* biology textbook and still convey the Biblical account of creation. State law doesn't require them to present both sides of the creation-evolution issue, but they feel it's important to do so. When they happen to be using a textbook that is heavily tilted toward evolution, they explain that evolution is only a theory, and creationism is an alternate theory. Then they read the creation accounts from the Bible (which I believe is a nondevotional use of the Bible in the classroom), and open the floor for discussion of *both* evolution and creation. They present both views as objectively as they can, in a manner that relieves peer pressure from Christian students who are being exposed to the theory of evolution for the first time. As a Christian parent, I would not worry about how that course would be taught after talking with one of these teachers. I know I can trust their "hidden curriculum."

3. Discuss With the Child. You may decide to approve a book that is partly objectionable, because it is the best book available on a given topic. Or the committee may choose a book that you find objectionable for a course that your child must take, and you have no alternative. Either way, discuss it with your child.

It's Worth the Trouble

By now you may be thinking, "This seems like more

trouble than it's worth! Why not let my school officials pick the textbooks by themselves? I can always complain if I don't like something."

Well, the textbook adoption process *can* require considerable effort. Much time and effort are required if the decisions are to be made properly. But if you have ever tried to remove a textbook series from the public schools *after* it's been adopted, *after* the school system has spent tens of thousands of dollars to put the material in place, you would realize that it's far less trouble for you to get involved *before* the textbooks are chosen. And there's far less emotional trauma.

I am going to share the experience of some parents who learned this lesson the hard way. I hesitate to share it, because I know they would like to put these bitter memories behind them. But I feel that I should share it, in the hope that you will learn from their tragedy.

The school board at Warsaw, Indiana was catapulted into the national news arena in 1977 when it withdrew a textbook series entitled, *Values Clarification,*[8] and discontinued that course at the high school. Several parents felt the school board had violated their children's First Amendment rights by making that decision. The decision was challenged in school board meetings and private confrontations between parents and board members.

The community began to choose sides. The parents who objected to this decision filed a lawsuit against the board. A reporter from the PBS network news program, *The MacNeil-Lehrer Report,* appeared at the school office to find out what was happening. One school official spent the entire day with this reporter, making a tour of the Warsaw schools. The reporter was so impressed that he decided not to file a report on the network news, to avoid giving the problem more publicity. But some parents supported the board's right to remove those materials, and they formed a citizen's committee to voice their opinion that *Values Clarification* should have been removed. The citizen's committee set out to examine other books in the Warsaw high school—textbooks, supplementary texts, and library books of all kinds. They added four other books to their "hit list."

One of these was the novel entitled, *Go Ask Alice* (by an anonymous author). The citizen's committee charged that the language in this book was blatantly obscene. Most people didn't believe that could be so. Why would the school board purchase an obscene book with their tax dollars? So the *Warsaw Times Union* decided to set the record straight. The newspaper published unabridged excerpts directly from the book. It was worse than many patrons in the community had imagined. I suppose you could have walked into a public restroom and copied some of the words right off the restroom walls. All the four-letter sexual obscenities were there, and the newspaper quoted them verbatim. It had a tremendous shock effect on the Warsaw community.

The school board managed to withdraw the *Man* series, *Go Ask Alice, Values Clarification,* and several other books. That might have been the end of the issue. Unfortunately, some of the books were given to members of a local senior citizens' group. They chose to place them in a wire basket at a public park and burn them in the presence of a newspaper photographer. The *Warsaw Times Union* printed a dramatic photo of that event—with the name "WARSAW" emblazoned across a park pavilion behind part of the flaming heap of textbooks—and the wire services carried that photo to newspapers around the world. (The photographer who took that picture said the foreign publications requested copies of it.) So it was that Warsaw, Indiana became known as a quiet little town where people like to burn textbooks.

Everyone in the Warsaw Community School District

became an unwitting victim of passion. There were no winners. The whole affair generated great hostility between the parents and their school officials. I am sure that teachers and principals who survived that ordeal feel defensive, even now, when they see certain parents enter the school building. That's tragic. But as I said, you can learn something from their experience.

Let me share an observation that George Van Alstine makes in his book, *The Christian in the Public Schools.* It's wise counsel for us as we get involved in any aspect of our children's public education; but I feel it's especially pertinent as we evaluate our children's textbooks. He says:

We cannot expect to become instant experts on complicated educational problems when others have already invested many hours trying to solve them. The Christian parent who comes on like a reformer with all the answers will be quickly and properly rejected. We need to do a great deal of listening and gathering of information before we will be able to contribute in a creative way.[9]

School officials will respect your opinion if they know that you have taken time to get the facts firsthand, and if you express your opinion in a calm and reasonable manner. Make that kind of reputation for yourself. Then offer to help select the next round of textbooks. You are more likely to be called.

NOTES

[1]The number of states with Textbook Adoption Committees will change nearly every year, as legislatures pass new laws. But currently there are twenty-two adoption states: Alabama, Arizona, Arkansas, California, Florida, Georgia, Hawaii, Idaho,

Indiana, Kentucky, Louisiana, Mississippi, Nevada, New Mexico, North Carolina, Oklahoma, Oregon, South Carolina, Tennessee, Texas, Utah, and Virginia. Most other states will allow local school boards to set up textbook committees, if they wish. But their book choices may be subject to state approval.

[2]A few states do *not* require citizen input on their local Textbook Adoption Committees; this policy also changes nearly every year, according to the sentiments of the legislators. Ask your principal or school superintendent about the current policy in your area.

[3]"Chapter 1" is the new name for the Federal educational aid program that formerly was called "Title 1." The name changed on July 1, 1982.

[4]Normally, the state Textbook Adoption Committee will screen out books with inferior binding, paper, or other problems. But if you question the durability or usability of the book in any way, note that on your checklist. You should mention it in your committee meeting. One state committee made the mistake of recommending an elementary school textbook with a white cover. The cover became horribly soiled in just a few weeks, but the students had to pass the books along for five more years. In another case, each teacher was supposed to tear a worksheet out of the books every week for the children to take home. But after a few pages were torn out, the binding came apart. State textbook committees do make mistakes—so be alert!

[5]Carl Sagan, *Cosmos* (New York: Random House, 1980), pp. 28-29, 337-339. Notice that I have cited *clear objections* to the book and *specific examples* of what I mean. You should be able to do the same with any book that you criticize before your committee.

[6]*Ibid.,* pp. 20, 53 ff., 78-79, 333.

[7]See "The Island Trees Decision" in Chapter 6 for details of a recent Supreme Court ruling on this issue.

[8]*Values clarification* is a phrase that educators use to refer to several different kinds of study, which are de-

signed to help students discover and clarify the moral values they already have. Students in a values clarification course might, for example, read a story and discuss whether they feel the characters "made the right decisions." They might draw pictures that portray some aspect of their lives, and explain what the pictures mean (a basic form of psychoanalysis). They might discuss conflicts they are having with their parents or their classmates, and try to find ways to resolve those conflicts (group psychotherapy). Many Christian parents object to the values clarification program because they feel it is an invasion of family privacy, and because it may reinforce a child's immature or distorted moral values.

[9]George Van Alstine, *The Christian in the Public Schools* (Nashville: Abingdon Press, 1982), pp. 93-94.

Volunteers

Much of America runs on volunteer energy—hospitals, mental health centers, the Red Cross, even the political system. The need for volunteers in our public schools is greater than ever before. Why? Pinched budgets! The federal government has pumped billions of dollars into public schools since the early 1960s, but those dollars are drying up. State and local funds are dwindling, too. Most schools need help! And Christians should view this as a tremendous opportunity to influence their public schools.

The federal government has just issued a formal invitation for you to get involved. Sandra Gray, executive director for the National School Volunteer Program, has said:

... More encouraging are the implications for school volunteerism in the next few years. As the embodiment of local, private initiative in a key social service arena, school volunteer programs are what this presidential administration is calling for in its campaign to reduce dependence on the public sector, especially the federal government. Thus, school volunteers will be more in demand than ever before. The vast reservoir of potential help and public support from business people, retired citizens, parents, and college students awaits.[1]

We Christians should recognize open doors of service, and this is one of them. The school volunteer program could allow us to fan out into more direct Christian service, such as holding "Good News Clubs" after school or organizing a Bible club during the school's club period. (See the chapter on "Prayer and Bible Reading.")

The parents of one of my former students have one of the most intense, direct, and effective Christian volunteer efforts that I've ever known. Here's how they did it:

Several years ago, the football coach who sponsored the Fellowship of Christian Athletes in our high school asked me (the choir director) to help him form a gospel singing group. For two years, the coach and I met with the young F.C.A. men who wanted to sing in this group. (We met in community homes once a week to rehearse our music and have a devotional time together.) It was a close-knit group with a real ministry to our community, as they sang in various churches on weekends.

Then I moved to another community and began work in a different school. So who was going to keep working with the gospel singing group?

The mother of a student came forward to volunteer. She was an accomplished pianist and a deeply committed Christian who had a genuine concern for teenagers. She was also confident enough to tackle the task of training these young athletes to sing! In 1974 she and her husband took charge of training the gospel singers; and today the group is larger and more effective than ever. They even performed at a national F.C.A. convention in Rome, Georgia a few years ago.

This couple never would have suspected that they would start working as school volunteers. But a need arose and they stepped forward to fill it. This is how most school volunteers get started.

Volunteers don't always make a teacher's job easier. But they do enable the teacher to accomplish more. If I am a teacher with thirty fourth-grade pupils, and I have a volunteer assisting me two hours each week, I need to prepare not only the lesson material for my pupils but also the assignments for my volunteer. I must assign to the volunteer whatever tasks I feel he or she can do. That frees me to do other things I ought to be doing with my class; but it certainly doesn't give me an "easy out" from my duties as a teacher.[2]

Getting Started

Perhaps your school does not yet have a volunteer program. So how could you get one established?

Well, I would *not* recommend unloading grandiose ideas on your principal. He or she has enough special projects already. But there are several ways you might plant the idea and help it grow:

1. *Find a need and fill it.* Look for a frustrated teacher who has too much to do, too many students, and far too little time. Perhaps the teacher has a handicapped pupil who needs special attention of some sort, or a few students who need some tutoring in math or reading skills. As a volunteer, you can give these students U.P.S.—unlimited personal service.

Ask the teacher if she would like some help for an hour or two each week. If she says "yes," then the next step (hurdle?) is to get the principal's approval. Remember the principal? That's the one you befriended at

142

the start of the school term, right? You or the teacher, or both, should approach the principal and see if he or she thinks it's OK for you to help the teacher in the specific ways you've agreed upon. The teacher will usually know how and when to approach the principal with this idea. When the time comes, assure the principal that other schools have used volunteers for several years; it is not a radically new idea.

After you've served as a volunteer for a month or so, you might tell the principal, "You know, my next-door neighbor wants to know if you could use another volunteer. Would it be all right for her to come in and try helping another of your teachers for awhile?"

The principal probably will say, "Sure!"

In that fashion, a volunteer program could evolve at your school over a length of time, as the needs of the school dictate.

2. *Contact the National School Volunteer Program and ask them to help you get started.* This organization is interested in expanding the use of adult volunteers in the public schools. They can provide ideas and practical guidelines for starting a volunteer program at your school. The address of the N.S.V.P. is 300 North Washington Street, 23, Alexandria, VA 22314.

3. *Ask your school officials to appoint a Director of Volunteer Services (D. V.S.).* The D.V.S. does not need to be a person with formal academic credentials. Sometimes a less sophisticated leader is willing to plunge ahead with innovative programs that we professional educators would fear to try. The D.V.S. should have a positive outlook on the work of the school. He or she should be a warm, accepting person who tries to understand how other people feel, and who wants to help others develop their full potential. The D.V.S. should have some organizational skill and be able to work as a pleasant "go-between" with volunteers and paid staff members.

Maybe this sounds like you. Then why not offer your

own services as the D.V.S.? Or suggest someone else in your community who seems to fill the bill. This key leader is often the one who "gets the ball rolling" with a school volunteer program.

When a volunteer program gets started at your school, you'll find that some teachers will want help right away—and others will not! Some teachers may feel threatened by volunteers, or they may feel that instruction is their solo responsibility. But, generally, even these insecure teachers will ask for volunteers after they see what volunteer workers have done for other teachers.

The volunteers may feel a bit apprehensive, too. Some may want to work only with kindergartners, because they're afraid they don't know enough to work with students at upper levels or will be unable to manage older children. Do you feel that way? Relax! I'll let you in on a secret—most children are still manageable. And 2 + 2 is still 4. The old rules of logic still apply. While you may not understand all the *content* of your students' lessons, you do understand how to work with people and help them learn. That's your most important contribution as a school volunteer.

I believe most teachers are good judges of ability. They seem to know, in most cases, just how much to ask of a volunteer. They can discern how many students you'll be able to manage at a time, and they don't try to overload you. (Of course, if you do feel overloaded, you can ask the teacher to change your work plans. And she will.)

What You'll Be Doing

Some mothers, when they first hear of the chance to work as a school volunteer, immediately think how nice it will be to work in their own child's classroom for a couple of hours each week. But that may not happen. Teachers who've used volunteer help sometimes feel

144

that it's unwise to assign a parent to his or her own child's classroom. That's especially true in the primary grades, where parents may become so engrossed with what their own son or daughter is doing that they neglect the other students.

When you tell your principal or one of the teachers that you'd like to work as a volunteer, you may be assigned to a classroom where your child is not involved. And you'll be asked to do *whatever* would help the teacher of that class the most. Be ready for anything—especially for a challenge!

When you become a volunteer, you may be asked to tie shoelaces, wipe runny noses, hold scissors, put on boots and snowsuits, prepare bulletin boards, run duplicating machines, chaperone field trips, read to students, assist slow learners with math or reading, help gifted students with special projects, or do any number of other things.

You might wonder, "Why do gifted students need help?" Because the teacher may have thirty students of average ability, and she cannot give time to challenge that gifted student to stretch his skills and take on special assignments. But a volunteer does have the time.

Recently, I discussed the needs of gifted students with a professor from Indiana University. She felt that it's not a good idea to pull gifted students out of the public school classroom and create a large, expensive program for all the gifted students of that school district. She believed it is best to keep the child with his friends. Recognize his special abilities and challenge him to use those abilities on special projects; but keep him in the regular classroom with others of average and even below-average ability. That's just one educator's opinion, of course, but I believe we will see more schools follow this pattern, especially as they run low on funds.

As a volunteer, you can give students personal attention that they might not receive otherwise. A volunteer recently told me how she was asked to take a group of kindergarteners across the hall to another work area, where they would do a counting exercise. Each child had a large sheet of paper with several boxes; each box had several dots. They were to count the total number of dots in all of the boxes. When they started this exercise, one of the boys came to the volunteer and said, "Mrs. Harper, would it be all right if I just plus 'em up?"

This little fellow already knew how to add! He was bored with this counting business! So the volunteer said, "Sure. Just plus 'em up." And when he had finished, she patted him on the back and gave him a word of praise. These kinds of things are less likely to occur in a group of thirty children.

The volunteer can take the pressure off a teacher who has problem children in her class. I periodically hear teachers express genuine frustration at this point. In a class of twenty-five to thirty children, the teacher may have a half a dozen aggressive children that are difficult to manage or several children with special needs. When a volunteer comes in to help the teacher—even if only once a week—he relieves a great emotional burden from the teacher. Each hyperactive or aggressive child can spend a half-hour or so with the volunteer, in one-to-one conversation, and find real emotional release of some of that pent-up energy. The volunteer may be able to meet the student's needs better in that half-hour session than the teacher could in a large group of students in a full week.

Individual Attention

This leads me to a key advantage of volunteer work: the advantage of individual attention. A school volunteer can give more time to the needs of individual students, more than the overworked teacher can. And this has many benefits.

146

For example, volunteers can accomplish much in the affective area of learning—in other words, dealing with the students' values and attitudes. One volunteer shared with me how she was working with a first-grade boy whose father had just died of cancer. Two weeks after the father's death, the mother was hospitalized. That was traumatic for the little boy. He'd seen his father spend much of the last year or so in the hospital, and he had died. Was his mother going to die, too? The volunteer sensed his fear, so she spent about half an hour with him, helping him vent his fears. Then she reassured him that his mother would probably be all right; she explained that most people who go to the hospital *do* get better. He needed to know that.

Volunteers aren't expected to be full-fledged counselors. Nor should they try to be. But they have many opportunities to assure and guide students' lives. For this reason, volunteer work provides an excellent way for Christians to be a "leaven" in our society.

Another volunteer was once practicing a list of vocabulary words with a second grader. The little girl was supposed to form a couple of sentences using each word on the vocabulary list, to show the volunteer that she knew what the words really meant. So they took the list out in the hallway to practice. In a little while, the girl used one of the words to form a sentence about Jesus; for the next couple of minutes, they had a conversation about Jesus. The volunteer was not proselytizing the girl. But she let the girl know that Jesus was important to her, too; and that was a very supportive experience for the girl.

A volunteer may be able to spot special problems that the teacher might not notice as she works with the whole class. For example, one volunteer noted that two children had a seepage from the ear. She reported these ear infections to the teacher, who relayed the information to the school office. The students were given medical help before the infection spread.

The time a child spends with a school volunteer is virtually the only time that some children have with an individual adult. This is not the fault of the teacher; obviously, no teacher could give thirty minutes or more to private sessions with every student every week. But many children have both parents working, or a single parent who works two jobs. These children need more time for one-to-one conversation with an adult than they can get at home. A school volunteer can provide that time.

A good volunteer will give students this kind of emotional support. Many students come from broken homes; some are neglected and abused by their parents; some have been told they are going to fail in school. A good volunteer helps these students regain their self-esteem. He helps them realize they are not second-rate human beings. He encourages them to develop the full potential God has given each one of them.

One volunteer worked with a boy for two years, spending a half hour each week with him, trying to overcome his lack of motivation. This boy constantly misbehaved in class. He kept stirring up trouble with the other students, and he would not concentrate on his work. But the volunteer encouraged him to study. She pointed out the great potential he had, if he would apply himself to the work.

Finally, the boy moved on to the next grade, and the volunteer had no more contact with him. Two years passed. Then one day she saw him in a local grocery store. He saw her, too. And he made a beeline to meet her.

"Hi, Mrs. Dunn!" he said with a smile. "I haven't seen you for a while! Guess what? I'm going to high school this fall!"

For several minutes, the youth engaged this lady in a friendly conversation. He was obviously different. His attitude toward school was much different. And he thanked her for the work she'd done with him. He said, "You're one of the best teachers I ever had."

Remember, this lady was *not* his teacher. She was a volunteer. But she had affected his emotional life more powerfully than any teacher he could remember.

Who Can Volunteer?

School volunteers come from all walks of life. They come in various ages. They come with various skills. But we need every one of them. Here are some examples of the kind of folks we need to volunteer for work in our classrooms:

1. *Parents.* Homemakers with school-aged children make excellent volunteers. Women whose husbands work, and who have all their children in school may have some free time, now—time they'd like to use productively. And the school volunteer program is a good way to do that.

But we need men volunteers as well as women. Many children live in a home with no father present. There may be no close relatives who provide a positive male image for these children. So when a Christian man comes to the classroom to do volunteer work for an hour each week, he can bring a very positive influence to the students. Especially if the school has few male teachers.

Nationwide we see a trend toward more flexible work hours. Not everyone works the traditional 9-to-5 schedule. Many men on "flex-time" are able to block out two hours or so every week to work as volunteers in their local schools. Even those who work the traditional second shift can work in the evening, sleep a full eight hours in the morning, and be available for a couple of hours in the early afternoon. This opens up some exciting possibilities for community service, such as doing volunteer work at the school.

2. *Retirees.* Yes, we need retiree volunteers. In our

mobile society, many children live hundreds—even thousands—of miles from their grandparents. They have no close association with any human being older than their parents. So there's real value in having retired folks come into the school classroom to work with students. They can bring a new perspective to life that the students would not get otherwise. This contact could reshape some young people's image of older adults. It could enrich the life of the volunteer retiree as well.

3. *Young single adults.* Many of these people work a second-shift or third-shift job, and they have time available for volunteer work in the daytime. They are energetic and creative. And they, too, can provide good adult models for the kids.

4. *Students.* Many communities have college or university campuses with students who major in education. These students can get practical experience in their field by working as school volunteers. (They can also find out whether they'll really like their chosen field!)

High school students may also be able to help, and their school officials may release them from other duties for a few hours each month to work as volunteers in nearby elementary schools. (Of course, we need to be cautious here; some students would jump at the chance to get out of study hall, but not take the volunteer task seriously. The high school principal or guidance counselor can usually tell which students are serious about this type of work.)

Even junior high students can do volunteer work. My own daughter was a student volunteer for two periods each week while she was in middle school. She was excused from study hall, walked to the other end of the building (where the elementary classes are held), and assisted a first-grade teacher. Liesl has decided that she wants to be a teacher. And that decision is now tempered by three years of limited but firsthand experience in the classroom. The first graders still look up to a middle school student with a bit of awe; they consider them good role models.

In one instance some seventh- and eighth-grade boys, who were giving some of their teachers trouble with discipline, were cautiously recruited as volunteers to work with first- and second-grade children. Their sense of duty to the children was exemplary. They honored the responsibility and trust that were given them, even though not all their behavior problems in the middle school were eliminated.

Ideas for Volunteer Programs

Earlier I said that one of the best ways to become a school volunteer is to find a need and fill it. So what are some needs that your school might have right now?

Perhaps your school is planning a play or musical sometime this year. They need costumes, background sets, and a hundred other things. You might have some special talents to help in these areas—sewing costumes, building sets, creating period hairdos, and so on.

Your school may not have anyone to teach physical education, music, or art. The financial crunch has caused many schools to reduce these programs or cut them out entirely. Some states (such as Nebraska and Wyoming) have relaxed their course requirements because they cannot afford to hire teachers for these special subjects. Why not offer to teach in one of these areas?

Your home or job may offer something special. One teacher in our school belongs to a black powder club whose members shoot muzzle loaders and wear buckskin costumes for special events. He has appeared in elementary schoolrooms with all his frontier regalia to explain how people lived in pioneer days.

One father who works in a textile mill called his son's

teacher and said, "How would you like to bring the class over for a tour of our plant?"

The teacher said, "That's a great idea! The students have never seen how cloth is made and dyed. It would give them a better idea of how we get the clothes we wear."

The father got approval from the plant supervisor, and they brought a busload of students to the plant for a full-fledged tour. The children loved it.

We live in a rural school district. Yet guest speakers from our community have included a former member of the White House staff, a retired F.B.I. agent, a state conservation officer, and a sheep farmer. Ask yourself, "Do I have something special to offer the students at my school? Will my experience have something of interest for them?" You might be surprised at what you have to share.

Here's another idea: Suppose you live in a school district with very small school libraries. This might be true in rural schools, in urban ghetto schools, or many other places. Why not get together with some other concerned Christian parents and create a mobile library? You could outfit a van with bookshelves and stock it with wholesome, informative books. You could drive it to the various schools in your district on a prearranged schedule, so students could check out the books. This would be a great summer activity!

Don Bagin of Glassboro State College points out the need for "key communicators" in your school.[3] These people serve as a volunteer "grapevine" for the school, ready to spread the word of what's happening at the school to other members of the community. For example, if school officials know that a lot of people in your community get their news from the barber and the beautician, they may ask those folks to serve as key communicators. If they know that Mrs. X likes to chat on the telephone with her friends, they may ask her to be a key communicator.

When there's a troublesome incident in the school, the principal calls these key communicators and says, "Here's something that happened at school today. People in the community will be hearing about it, I'm sure. But I want you to have the straight facts about what happened, and put out the word about how we dealt with it."

Mr. Bagin gives the example of a fight between a black student and a white student, ninth graders. Because the black student had caused several other disturbances at the school, the principal suspended him; but since it was the white student's first offense, he was not suspended. The principal called his key communicators and explained the situation to them. They put out the news to their community. There was no riot. There was no protest. I'd venture to say that some of the black leaders of the community even would have commended the principal for what he did. But he made sure everyone got the story straight the first time.[4]

Here are some guidelines that may help you become an effective school volunteer:

1. *Be prompt in your arrival time.* Your teacher must be able to depend on you. If you must cancel your participation for some reason, let the teacher know as soon as you can.

2. *Know and follow school policies.* Some schools have special guidelines for their volunteers. Even if they don't they do have guidelines for the conduct of their regular teachers; follow those guidelines. Don't assume you have special privileges because you're a volunteer.

3. *Dress modestly.* I'll not presume to tell you what your standard of dress should be; you ought to know what is appropriate for your community. Obviously, you should not dress extravagantly, eccentrically, or seductively.

4. *Do not divulge personal information about the children with anyone outside the classroom.* When you

work as a volunteer, you will be privy to much personal information about the students and their families. Consider that information a sacred trust. Don't go home and say to your spouse, "Do you know what Mr. Brown did last night?" You will be effective as a school volunteer only so long as the students, teachers, and the parents can trust you.

5. *Have a positive attitude.* A teacher may assign you to a student who is slow and struggling with his work. That student may already have a self-defeated outlook, very low self-esteem. So don't make him feel worse. Be a reinforcer, an encourager, an optimist about the student's prospects for learning. It can be contagious.

During cut-and-paste time in a kindergarten class, one little boy leaned over and cut the ear of another boy with his scissors. Blood flowed. Tears flowed. It was a traumatic moment for the whole class. The next day the first volunteer arrived in the classroom early and peered around the door—wearing earmuffs! The teacher laughed. And that gag was enough to ease the tension in the class for the rest of the day.

6. *Don't bring your own preschool children to the classroom with you.* That should go without saying. But you'd be surprised how often some school volunteers bring a busy little three-year-old along!

7. *Pray for the teacher and students with whom you work.* Volunteer work is a ministry. It's one way in which you can serve other people in the spirit of Christ. So pray for the people you serve.

8. *Don't proselytize.* While you ought to manifest a Christian attitude and uphold Christian standards in what you do, you should not see your volunteer work as "soul-winning." A student may ask you about your beliefs. If so, feel free to share them briefly. But don't make your tutoring sessions evangelism sessions; that's not your purpose for being in the school. If you do so, you could jeopardize your volunteer participation. In fact, you could place an entire program in peril.

A Channel for Involvement

As government funds for education become tighter, I believe the school volunteer movement will spread. It will become a channel for parents to become actively involved in the daily life of their schools. And this can only be constructive in the long run.

A principal from a neighboring school district visited me recently to ask how he might start a volunteer program at his school. After I'd shared some specific ideas, he said, "I'm not so sure this is going to work. The parents want a volunteer program, but the teachers are leery of it. They remember how the parents pressured them to remove a certain reading program from our school a few years ago. They still have bitter memories of that."

When I asked him what he thought of that particular reading program, he said that he didn't think it belonged in the school either. He was pleased that the school no longer used that program.

"Then why are you afraid of the parents?" I asked. "It seems to me that they helped you eliminate a problem that you might not have been able to eliminate yourself."

"Well, okay," he said with a smile. "Guess I hadn't looked at it that way."

The unfortunate note in his situation was that early involvement by parents, and other concerned citizens of the community, likely would have prevented the implementation of such a program at the outset, and it would have spared the hurt feelings of many parents and school personnel.

Who knows? Maybe the government budget cuts are a blessing in disguise. Maybe the cuts will constrain our schools to draw in people from the community more eagerly than ever. If so, I believe the school volunteer program is in the mainstream of better things for our public schools.

NOTES

[1]Sandra Gray, *The Volunteer in Education* (Alexandria, VA: National School Volunteer Program, 1981).

[2]There is an important difference between a school volunteer and a teacher's aide. An aide is someone *hired* by the school to assist the teacher of a large class; some teachers' unions require that an aide be hired when a teacher's class reaches a given size. The aide is a member of the school staff, on the payroll, and directly accountable to the principal. The volunteer is not a member of the staff. He or she is a person from the community who's offered to help a particular teacher with a particular task. While the volunteer is accountable to the principal, he or she is primarily responsible to the teacher. (And the volunteer is not on the payroll.)

[3]Ethel Herr, *Schools: How Parents Can Make a Difference* (Chicago: Moody Press, 1981), pp. 199-203.

[4]*Ibid.*, pp. 200-201.

The School Board

Let's say you're really upset about something that's happening in your school. You're steamed. And you think, "I'm going to go to the next school board meeting and give them a piece of my mind!"

Well, you certainly can. You're legally entitled to meet with the school board. And sometimes you *must*. But parents often misunderstand how a school board operates, and they have unrealistic hopes of what they can accomplish in a major showdown with the board. Parents are tempted to think that if they make the loudest explosion, they'll be heard. But that's not necessarily true.

Let's take a moment to think about your local school board. Let's try to understand what makes the board "tick." As we do, I think you'll get a better idea of how to influence the school board without making yourself their adversary.

How a School Board Operates

School boards vary in their number of members. A small board may have only five members or so, while the board of a large metro district may have more than a dozen members. Many school boards are elected. In some districts, each board member represents a particular area—a borough or township—while others may be elected "at large" to represent the entire district. Some school boards are appointed by the local city officials.

Educators have long debated whether the elected or the appointed school board is better. I've heard parents appointed to a city school board say, "Oh, it's so political!" Well, don't let anyone convince you that a small town elected school board *isn't* political too! Politicians may contend for a seat on the school more vigorously than they fight for any other office; they may consider the school board a political "plum." Though most school board members get paid very little, they wield considerable influence over the affairs of the community; so the local political leaders vie for control of the board. And, of course, a seat on the school board can make a convenient launching pad to a more ambitious political career.

Some candidates run for the school board because they have an ax to grind. They disagree with the way some administrator or teacher is handling things, and they have vowed to set things in order. They tell the voters, "Elect me and I'll get rid of the troublemakers."

Some run for the school board because they genuinely care about their schools. While they see many things wrong with the school system, they also see great potential there. They believe they can influence the schools for good. They may be naive in that hope; they may expect to do some things that they just can't do with the schools. But they have honest intentions.

In some small districts, a person may run for the

school board on the simple policy, "We will not raise taxes! We will not raise teachers' salaries! The superintendent is overpaid already! Elect me, and I will save you thousands of tax dollars." That promise will get some folks elected to the board.

Some rural school districts are still under the township trustee system, in which the elected trustees serve on the school board in addition to many other duties (such as dispensing welfare aid). The trustee system may be intensely political. The trustee wields considerable power over a wide range of school policies—from teachers' salaries to bus routes. The trustee can be a benevolent dictator. Instead of consulting with a group of other officials about what to do, he can simply announce, "This is going to be our policy beginning tomorrow at nine o'clock." So decisions can be made very swiftly under the trustee system; but often, the wrong things happen swiftly.

Boards vary a great deal in their psychological makeup. Some boards are quite dictatorial; they try to control every decision and make their school superintendent a puppet. At the other extreme is a school board that is virtually a puppet or rubber stamp of the superintendent. They say, "You're the professional educator. Whatever you say is best, we'll do it." Some school boards callous themselves against public opinion; they don't seem to care what the public thinks. At the other extreme is a school board so eager to please that they blow with the wind; whenever someone walks into their meeting and complains, the board jumps to change their policy.

If you're part of a large city school system, you may yearn to live in small towns because you think there would not be so much political maneuvering. But you would be surprised if you knew what happens in some of those small towns. In the late 1960s, the school board members of a small town in central Indiana found their telephones out of order one morning. The head of the local telephone company didn't get his way in the town board meeting the night before, so he simply retaliated by cutting off the board members' phone service. As you can imagine, that caused an uproar!

What does a school board do? Well, to put it in the simplest terms, the school board sets school policy.

Budget. A school board, in consultation with their superintendent of schools or school business manager, will review school budgets and set teachers' salaries. They may be able to control the local tax rate, if the state legislature has not put a ceiling on it. They decide what percentage of the tax money will go to salaries, what part for construction, what part for instructional materials, and so on.

Salaries. Closely related to the board's budgetary power is the school board's control over teacher's salaries. Nearly every local school board sets its own teachers' salaries. And this often brings the board into strong conflict with teachers' unions. Most school boards have to deal with teacher negotiation committees—they even make use of full-time negotiators.

Hiring and Firing. The board may delegate this responsibility to their superintendent or a principal; nevertheless, no one is really hired on a school staff until the board approves. The superintendent may interview a prospective teacher, for example, and be very impressed with her or his credentials. But he will close the interview by saying, "I'll present your contract to the board next week for their approval."

Facilities. Many school boards are having to decide whether to close certain buildings and sell them. School enrollments have declined for several years; some buildings are only partially full. Yet when a board tries to consolidate a couple of schools and close down the half-empty building, they may arouse a great deal of hostility in the community. Parents don't like to see a board phase out the school they attended. The board has that power, though.

Curriculum. The school board is the final authority for determining the curriculum of a school. They decide whether art courses will be taught, for example. They decide whether specially certified teachers will be hired for such a course, or whether the regular classroom teacher will handle it. They decide what sort of physical education program each school may have. They decide whether the schools will offer one foreign language, or three, or none. (Unless the state mandates otherwise.)

Transportation. The school board decides whether they will have single bus routes or double bus routes; which students will be eligible to ride the bus; how the schools will comply with federal busing orders; and so on.

Schedule. The school board determines the length of the school day. Again, the state legislature or State Board of Education may set some requirements in this area. The state may require that students be in class for *so many hours* each week; but the local school board has wide latitude to determine how they will achieve that total.

Food Service. The federal government mandates the basic nutritional requirements for a school lunch program. Washington calls for so many ounces of carbohydrates, so much protein, etc., in every week's school lunch menu. But the local board controls the purchasing of food for the lunch program, the hiring of cooks, and so on.

Whenever a school board votes on an issue, their meeting must be open to the public. However, the board need not *discuss* the issue in public; they can go into executive session, bar all spectators from the room, and discuss a matter behind closed doors before they take a vote. This is often desirable.

No one seems to like private meetings except those who are in the meeting. However, school boards must sometimes discuss sensitive personal matters which would only become community gossip if made public.

Many school districts require the building principals or personnel offices to appear before the school board and provide an evaluation report on their teachers and other employees.

A principal may be working with a particular teacher who is not doing a good job. The teacher has received poor evaluations, with several specific areas listed that need improvement. The principal has made the teacher aware that lack of sufficient progress may mean termination of employment after one more year.

The teacher needs to know this. The school board needs to know this. But the adults and students in the community do not need to know that this teacher's job is in jeopardy. He must still be given the opportunity to do the best job he is capable of without neighborhood gossip interference.

The following year this teacher's performance will again be discussed in a private meeting. If he is not to be rehired, this formal action will take place in a public school board meeting, and the action will be a matter of public record. You may have a gallery of a thousand people listening when the teacher is dismissed, though the specifics of the case were discussed in private.

This is true of hiring, firing, budget adoption, opening bids for construction projects, or any other legal action of the board: The action vote must be taken in an open meeting. The decision must be a matter of public record.

This means that you have an opportunity to know every action your school board takes. It also means that you know how your own board representative voted on a given issue. So if you're dissatisfied with how a certain board member has acted, you can complain to him. And if you're still not satisfied, you can work to unseat him in the next election.

Yes, you have many opportunities to see what the

board is doing. And you have opportunity to run for election for appointment to the board. You can affect board policy from the inside. Don't neglect that opportunity, if you feel strongly that your board needs to change direction.

How You Can Influence Your Board

Christian parents can have a beneficial influence on school board meetings. Unfortunately, many Christian parents come to a board meeting only when they're ready for a blowup. They have not gotten involved with their school boards until they wanted a heavy confrontation—and then they got what they wanted! A lot of people have been wounded and embittered by that kind of battle. A school board meeting lends itself to a heavy confrontation, because the atmosphere is charged, the media is present, and it's where a lot of heavy decisions are being made.

A school board meeting also lends itself to grandstanding by someone who wants attention. Things are not always the way they seem to be. Several years ago a patron in a neighboring school district began attending school board meetings on a regular basis. He soon became stridently vocal against many things the board was doing. He said the bus routes were not right and were wasting money; the principals should not have raises because it might affect the local tax rate; the student textbook rental fees were too high; and he didn't see why money had to be budgeted for teacher and administrator conferences. After all, these cost money and everyone knows that they are just all-expense-paid vacations anyway.

He went on this way week after week, until he filed to run for county commissioner. Then he stopped coming to the meetings. He had accomplished his purpose—he used the school board meeting and the media to establish the idea that if he were elected as county commissioner he would be their watchdog for the dollar. He had manipulated others into giving him considerable free publicity through the public forum of the local school board meeting.

I have not seen many wise Christians in school board meetings. But I believe that has been the result of ignorance; parents simply didn't know how to bring about the changes they wanted, in a constructive way.

A lot of people who want to make changes that Christian parents *disapprove* of—such as sex education, values clarification, and the like—must make their case before the school board. So Christian parents should at least be aware of what the school board is doing. (The school board itself may not be aware of what it's doing. In the case of a new curriculum course, for example, the board often adopts what a committee of teachers and/or principals recommended to it. They are often not aware of specific course content. They may not realize the impact of a values clarification course or an explicit sex education course until someone calls their attention to it!)

Most often Christian parents work out their school problems on a one-to-one basis with a teacher or a principal and do not find it necessary to come to the school board. But if you've tried that route and still feel you ought to meet with the school board, I'd suggest that you call your school superintendent ahead of time. Don't just march in and surprise people with your complaint; if you do, they're not likely to be greeted warmly. (You do want them to be receptive, don't you? You want them to *act* on your complaint.)

Just call your school system's central office and say, "May I speak to the superintendent, please?" Unless you live in Chicago, Los Angeles, or some other large metro district, you will probably be able to have that kind of access to your school superintendent. (If you do live in a metro district, you may have to go through more red tape. You may be shunted to several of the

164

superintendent's subordinates before you get an interview. But be persistent. You'll still be able to air your feelings to the board.)

Explain your concern to the superintendent. Most superintendents are masters at public relations; they'll listen! And they'll try to salve your wounds, if they can. Naturally they don't want a confrontation at the board meeting.

Let's say you present your case to the superintendent, and the superintendent is not able to deal with your concern. He or she arranges for you to appear before the next meeting of the school board. Is it wise for you to invite other concerned parents to attend?

I say yes. Your friends should not come to picket the board meeting or make a loud demonstration. Yet if a hundred people come in support of you when you stand before the board for five minutes, the board will know you are not speaking only for yourself. The local news media will be at the board meeting, and they are sure to note the presence of several who felt this way. The news report will say something like: "Mrs. So-and-So spoke to the board concerning this issue and there was a large gallery of people in support of this idea. The board tabled the motion until next month."[1]

Should you contact some board members in advance, to begin presenting your case? It depends. This can be very misleading. You might call one or two board members and get a very favorable response to your idea, so you think, "This is how the whole board feels. I don't really need to appear at the board meeting." But one or two members can't speak for the entire board. In fact, all of the members polled individually don't give you a fair reading of how they will think when they meet together. Or the opposite may be true: The members you contact by phone may be very unresponsive to you, and you might think it's hopeless to put your appeal to the whole board. But when they meet together, they might be ready to listen.

Of course, you may ruin your own cause if you make phone contacts with the board members beforehand. If you call a board member who doesn't like your idea, he's apt to contact the other members and do *his own groundwork* before the meeting. He'll say, "Mrs. Jones is coming to meet with us, and she's loaded for bear." So the board will be on the defensive when you meet with them.

In some instances, when a board has to consider a particularly thorny issue, they form a district-wide advisory committee to study the problem. These committees might have from twenty to sixty people—many of them parents—doing an in-depth study of the problem at hand. The committee might take polls of the citizenry, might compare the local school budget with the budgets of nearby districts, might interview local business leaders to set some long-range goals for the schools, and so on. This committee can provide an effective bridge between the school board and local parents, when dealing with "heart" issues. You could suggest that the board form such a committee to study the question you've raised, if it seems especially ticklish.

What You Can—and Can't—Expect

Every parent has a right to be heard. Every parent has a right to use the political system to influence the schools. But no parent has the right to expect that the board will grant his every wish.

Christian parents should become part of the process. They should try to influence the policies of their school system. But they should realize they have no right to expect that the system will always run the way they want.

Because the school system *is* a political system, I would like to see parents express their views concerning the schools as they do about any other political issue, without school officials getting on the defensive.

But for some reason, some school officials seem to feel their policies are above question. The people at City Hall expect citizens to challenge what they do, as part of the political process; but school officials sometimes don't.

I believe this situation can be changed. I believe it *will* be changed as concerned parents begin talking with their school boards. When parents make their wishes known in a reasonable, intelligent way, school boards will realize that parents respect them. That's when constructive decisions can be made.

NOTES

[1]Of course, you have to read some media reports with a bit of skepticism. I have attended school board meetings and then read the newspaper account of those meetings the next day, and wondered if I was really there! Reporters tend to focus on controversial issues. You may have a half-hour discussion of school curriculum—good, healthy brainstorming about what the board should do about certain subjects to be taught in the schools. And then there may be a two-minute discussion about the varsity basketball coach, some complaint about something the coach has done, and one of the board members makes a cutting remark about him. The newspaper report may give the headline and three lead paragraphs to the controversy over the coach, giving you the impression that it dominated the meeting. And the discussion of curriculum may be mentioned only in passing, or not at all. (Another good reason to attend board meetings! If, as Will Rogers said, "All you know is what you read in the papers," you may be grossly misinformed about what your board is doing!)

Prayer and Bible Reading

We all know that it is not legal for anyone to pray or read the Bible in a public school. Right? Well, I hope that by now enough has been said and written about his topic that you know the Supreme Court decisions of 1962/1963 were *not* that sweeping in purpose. But in case you haven't heard, let me emphasize the fact:

The United States Supreme Court has banned only two things from the public schools—*required* Bible reading and *mandatory* prayer. In other words, the Supreme Court has ruled that a school cannot *impose* Bible reading and prayer upon its students.

But, as a result, many schools have tried to remove all vestiges of religion. They have tried to ban all activities that might be construed as being religious.

This is an overreaction to the Court's decisions. The Supreme Court never intended for the schools to expel everything that might have religious overtones. As Christian attorney John Whitehead says, "The Constitution separated the institution of the church from the institution of the state, but not the Christian religion from the state nor Christians from meaningful activity within the state and society."[1]

Point of Law

The First Amendment says, "Congress shall make no law respecting an establishment of religion, or prohibiting the free exercise thereof." Notice that there are two distinct parts to this statement. The first is called *the establishment clause,* and the second part is called *the free exercise clause.*

The establishment clause declares that our government cannot create or set up a national religion. The free exercise clause guarantees that each individual is free to express his own religion—whether or not we agree with that religion. The fellow who wants to wear sackcloth and carry a placard down Main Street has the right to do so. The student who wants to bow his head has the right to do that, too. But can several students meet to pray? I believe they can because the Constitution guarantees them the right to free exercise of their religion and the right to peaceably assemble. But the American Civil Liberties Union would disagree. So would some civil attorneys.

A recent court decision upholding the Equal Access Act may be an issue of contention in coming months or years. "That law, enacted last year, prohibits public high schools that receive federal aid from barring student gatherings of their religious, political, or philosophical nature."[2] This means that school doors which are open to any type of group must be open to all groups, including those which are clearly religious in their intent. This does not, of course, allow them to do anything which would disrupt routine educational activities.

In 1962 and 1963, the United States Supreme Court rendered two decisions which have been embroiled in this controversy. In the Engel decision (1962), they struck down a twenty-two-word prayer which New York public school students recited. In the Shemp case (1963), the Court declared unconstitutional the Pennsylvania schools' practice of reading Bible verses over the school P.A. system each morning, and having the students' recite the Lord's Prayer. The Court never intended to remove the worship of God, the reading of Scripture, or voluntary prayer from the public schools. Following the Engel decision, Supreme Court Justice Thomas Clark said: "Most commentators suggested that the Court had outlawed religious observances in the public schools when, in fact, the Court did nothing of the kind."[3] In a college commencement address a couple of years later, Justice Clark added that "the Court has specifically held only one thing with specific reference to prayer in the public schools, and that is that a required prayer in the public schools violates the Constitution."[4]

Granted, many people disagreed with Justice Clark. Many still do. They would say that he is oversimplifying what the Court did. But I think a careful reading of the Engel and Shemp decisions will back up what he's said.

The Supreme Court took this action because *mandatory* prayer and *mandatory* Bible reading in tax-supported schools violates the Constitution. Evangelical Christians may suspect that the justices felt prayer and Bible reading just isn't that important to young people. But the Constitution was at stake. As Justice Clark pointed out, prayer and Bible reading *are* important. But since the schools are government agencies, they can't require students to pray or read the Bible in a devotional setting. We need to keep this clearly in mind.

The Supreme Court recently ruled that one state's moment-of-silence law was constitutional; yet the ruling prohibited moments of silence if students are told they may pray during that time. Two dozen states now have moment-of-silence laws. The court did not rule that these offend the Constitution, but that a teacher who suggests to students that they might pray during the moment of silence is actively promoting religion.

Of course, the Civil Liberties Union has hailed this decision as a major victory in keeping religion out of the schools, while activist Christians are condemning it as a deplorable act against the nation's heritage. This pot of controversy will continue to boil as long as there are public schools.

We seem to think that everything in the legal profession is either black or white; but that's not true. There are many gray areas in legal interpretation. Get a group of attorneys together and ask their opinion on a given legal question, and you'll find a wide variety of views. This certainly is true of the Court rulings on First Amendment rights in the public schools. But Justin Clark gets to the heart of the matter, I believe. The Supreme Court ejected *mandatory* prayer and Bible reading from the schools; and it should have.

A public school should not make worship a part of its curriculum. But that's exactly what some schools were doing.

What If the Court Hadn't Acted?

If you are a conservative, evangelical, Protestant Christian parent, you would not want a teacher to lead your children in a liturgical prayer every day. You wouldn't want your children to say so many "Hail Marys" at the start of class. But if prayer or devotional study became a formal part of the schools' curriculum, the teacher might lead your children in a prayer or Bible study that strongly clashed with your convictions.

So the Court showed real wisdom here. By banning mandatory prayer and Bible reading, they protected your right to bring up your children in the way you believe is right.

Prominent atheists such as Madalyn Murray (O'Hair) used those rulings to focus the spotlight on atheism. They polarized the situation. To their way of thinking, every school's program had to be atheistic; that was the only "patriotic" thing to do. Mrs. O'Hair felt that any teacher who mentioned God was violating the Constitution. Once she began her assault on the schools, principals felt they had to remove activities that would in fact have been permitted by the courts. They dreaded bad publicity. No more Christmas carols. No more bulletin-board pictures of the Pilgrims in prayer at Thanksgiving time.

But the Bible did not have to be removed from the public schools. Only its *mandated* used had to be ended. Prayer was not banned from the schools; only prescribed prayers were banned.

Why We Should Teach Bible in Our Schools

In my opinion, the Bible may and should be used in the public school curriculum. But we're not doing that. I think we're falling far short of providing a basic education for our young people, because we are not using the Bible.

Whole civilizations have been founded upon the moral principles contained in the Bible. It's cited frequently in our government documents, and in great literature such as the plays of Shakespeare. You really can't understand much of our Western culture unless you understand the Bible.

By what narrow vision of education do we devise a

school curriculum and omit the most popular Book of all time, a Book of tremendous literary and historical significance, a Book whose content has been the foundation of a multitude of nations down through the centuries?

How can we call students "educated" who have never been exposed to the Bible?

Dr. Northrop Frye of Indiana University says, "The Bible forms the lowest stratum in the teaching of literature. It should be taught so early and so thoroughly that it sinks straight to the bottom of the mind, where everything that comes along later can settle on it."[5] This man is speaking from a purely secular standpoint, and says that the Bible is the most important book that has ever been written. He doesn't recommend using the Bible because of its spiritual value, but because of its *intellectual* value. How can we deny our students the education that Scripture provides?

A high school English teacher in New York City named Joyce Vedral once had a meeting with her department chairman. They were concerned because the students seemed bored by their traditional English classes. Kids were "cutting classes" and neglecting their assignments. So what could they do? Joyce said—in desperation, really—"Why don't we try to offer a Bible class?"

The chairman said, "Sure. Go ahead."

So Miss Vedral drew up a curriculum plan for the class, had it approved, and began to publicize the fact that Bible would be offered the following term. They gathered the English students in one classroom to hear the announcement. She writes:

The morning I was to approach the students, I prayed for the right words. There I stood before the first of many classes and said, "I'm here to offer you a new course in place of regular senior English—The Bible as Literature."

The students groaned, gasped, and giggled.

I continued, "Many of you will be going to college. You will find the Bible is frequently quoted in English literature. Poetry is filled with references to it. So are novels and plays."

I stopped for a moment. The class was quiet. "Who can tell me who the first slaves in the Bible were?"

Silence.

"Who built the ark?" A few hands went up.

I could sense interest building.

"Do you know what the Bible says about how the world will end?"

They sat up.

"Do you know what the Bible says about witchcraft and fortune-telling?"

Now the students became noisy with students discussing the questions, speculating about the answers.

"This is not going to be a Sunday School class," I said. "We can discuss and even argue about religion. You can laugh and take it as a joke. That is your affair. My point is simply this: Do you want to be an educated person? If so, then how can you not know a little about the best-known book in the world?"[6]

When Miss Vedral had finished recruiting among twelve other classes, sixty students had signed up for Bible One.

Also, I think it's unfortunate that we don't start teaching Bible as literature until students reach high school. It really ought to be a part of the elementary school and junior high curriculum as well. There's too much valuable information in the Bible to be squeezed into a one-semester class during the senior year of high school. The traditional Bible stories of the Old

Testament teach social values just as well as the "Dick and Jane" and Dr. Seuss stories that elementary children read now. And the better Bible storybooks are written on such a level that they would certainly not run counter to the teaching of reading skills.

Let's Claim Our Privileges!

There is some freedom to engage in Christian activities in connection with the public schools, if we will avail ourselves of that freedom. We Christians need not be so afraid of exercising our privilege of being Christians! It is *not* unusual for Christian students to practice their beliefs on a public school campus—to engage in Bible study, in Christian service activities, and so on. And it's reasonable to expect that Christian students may continue to do that, as long as it doesn't infringe on other students' free exercise of their beliefs, or disrupt the educational processes of the schools.

I attended an elementary school that had about sixty students. During nice weather, we would congregate on the front steps every morning; someone would hoist the flag; and all the students would say the pledge of allegiance, sing "The Star-Spangled Banner," and pray.

My teacher marked off three columns on his chalkboard—"PLEDGE," "NATIONAL ANTHEM," and "PRAYER." A student could sign up for leading any of these activities, and we took turns doing it. It was simple. It was straightforward. I'm sure it had a positive effect on many of those children. But it was unconstitutional.

Not many of the parents in that community would have vocally objected to that practice, even if they disagreed with it. A person was either interested in the Christian faith or just didn't care; but no one was hostile. No longer is that true. Atheists and secular humanists of every sort are now quite vocal in protesting religious activities in the schools. Yet our courts are still interpreting the law rather broadly.

Some court decisions in recent months concerning Christmas observance, etc., have gone in favor of schools that want to observe these holidays. The courts have ruled that Christmas, Easter, and Thanksgiving are a part of our cultural tradition; they are not simply religious observances. Schools may go ahead and have their students sing, "Silent Night," for example. The A.C.L.U. doesn't like that. But the courts have been rather consistent at this point.

Prayer Is Permitted, If . . .

An article in *Education USA* magazine notes that prayer in the public schools must meet three tests to be allowed by the Supreme Court: (1) "It must have a secular purpose," (2) "its primary effect must be neither to advance nor inhibit religion," and (3) "the activity must not foster an excessive state entanglement with religion."[7] Some of these seem a bit absurd; I don't know how a person can have "secular" prayer, for example, because any prayer is an act of worship. But these technicalities are not of great concern to me. No court can keep a child from praying if he wants to pray. And no American court would want to prevent an individual teacher or child from praying. (Someone has said, "As long as teachers give tests, students will pray!")

Christian Clubs in the Schools

When it's a question of whether an organized group can meet in Room 101 for prayer time on Monday morning, the courts do get involved. And generally they have ruled that organized, officially sanctioned worship is unconstitutional in the schools. Christian groups such as Campus Life, or Fellowship of Christian Athletes will often be found having their meetings in students' homes in the evening rather

176

than meeting during the daytime on school property. Some schools allow students to meet on school property after school hours, as other special-interest clubs do.

The Fifth Circuit Court of Appeals ruled in March 1982 that the Lubbock, Texas school board could not permit such clubs to meet. The Lubbock Civil Liberties Union charged that students should not be allowed to meet for "any educational, moral, religious or ethical activities" in these clubs, even if "attendance at such meetings is voluntary."[8] The federal court agreed. The school board appealed this decision to the U.S. Supreme Court; but the Court refused to hear their appeal.

This ruling disturbs evangelical Christian parents. In fact, it should disturb all parents. Its scope is so far-reaching that it would ban *all* extracurricular meetings, except purely social gatherings. If it stands, it would spell the end of the Fellowship of Christian Athletes, Campus Life, Young Life—but also 4-H, drama clubs, honor societies, and anything else that falls under the verdict's sweeping indictment. So I think parents will press for legislation to override the Lubbock decision. Note this comment from Bob Sperlazzo, who has started Bible clubs at two high schools in Chicago. Bob has done considerable research into the Court's rulings at this point:

The Supreme Court ruled that students are free to express themselves on the [school] campus as long as the expression doesn't disrupt the orderly operation of the school and doesn't violate the rights of others. If the students meet these two requirements, then any interference on the part of the school officials is overstepping permissible Constitutional bounds. And the Court said that if the school officials are concerned that an outside speaker's lecture may create the feeling that the school system endorses his message, then the school can remedy this situation by requiring that before and after the presentation, an announcement be made that the school doesn't endorse it.[9]

In the case of a Bible club, or some other Christian club, there is no disruption of school activities. These meetings take place alongside other student club meetings. School officials should feel very free to allow a Bible club or some other Christian group to meet, even though they may choose to make a statement of disclaimer.

This is much different from the release-time plan, in which church leaders say to the school officials, "We'd like you to dispense with your planned classes at two o'clock every Wednesday so we can take your students out to a trailer and give them some Bible training." School officials often resist this idea. Rightly so.

We do an educational disservice, as well as a spiritual disservice, to our Christian students if we don't allow them to meet with other Christians and talk about things that are of special interest to them. Child Evangelism Fellowship, for instance, can have a great impact on elementary school students. If a Christian teacher is concerned about her children, and she lives in the community, she might start a local chapter of C.E.F. She would have club meetings for the children after school—at her own home or on school property, as with Campus Life or the F.C.A.

In our own school right now, we have a chapter of the Fellowship of Christian Athletes and Campus Life meets weekly in students' homes. The F.C.A. has a faculty sponsor and meets on a rotating basis with other clubs in the school. They are not a threat to anyone. No one in the community feels defensive or hostile about the existence of those clubs. They don't disrupt the educational process, nor are the students who attend those clubs ridiculed by anyone else. It's just a very natural part of the school week. Many of our students also participate in Campus Life as an outside-of-school activity.

In my opinion, a school should permit the Christian group to meet even if a leader from outside the school is in charge of it. For example, if a group of students asked a youth minister from a local church to form a Bible club at the school, I believe the school shouldn't deny that. Other outside leaders are permitted to lead students' groups. So if school officials allow outsiders to use the school building for other club activities, I think they should not forbid someone to use the building for religious club activities.

By the same token, a group of students could come to their principal with a request to start an occult club. Christian parents will be angered to think that a group meets just down the hall with black candles, crystal balls, and incantations. But it could happen. It's part of the price we pay for living in a free society.

Prayer and Bible reading in the public schools has been a hot issue in the 1980 and 1984 Presidential campaigns. Well-known evangelists hit the issue hard, week after week. Congress has debated various school prayer amendments (the most recent being introduced on March 3, 1984) and other bills designed to "put God back into the public schools." But God has never been pushed completely out of the schools. The freedom to worship and pray and read Scripture has never been withdrawn from public school students. We ought to realize that. And we ought to encourage our sons and daughters to keep on exercising the privileges they have.

NOTES

[1]John Whitehead, "The Secularizing of America," *Moody Monthly,* July-August 1981, p. 20.

[2]"Justice to Rule on Voluntary Student Religious Meetings in Schools," by Philip Hager, *Los Angeles Times,* February 10, 1985, p. 10.

³Jon Barton and John Whitehead, *Schools on Fire* (Wheaton, IL: Tyndale House, 1980), pp. 78-79.

⁴*Ibid.*, p. 79.

⁵*Ibid.*, p. 121.

⁶Joyce L. Vedral, "Here's What We're Doing," *Moody Monthly,* January 1977, p. 54. For other examples of how the Bible is being taught in the public schools, see "There's a Place for God in Room 101," by Lenore Derfelt, *Moody Monthly,* September 1981, pp. 34-36.

⁷"School Prayers Must Pass Three Tests," *Education USA,* February 8, 1982, p. 193.

⁸"Lubbock Prayer Plan Rejected," *Church and State,* May 1982, p. 19.

⁹"How to Get into the Public Schools without a Lawsuit," *The Christian Citizen,* April 1981, p. 29.

A Plan
for Action

We are a fragmented society. Dozens of special-interest groups are pushing, pulling, fighting, and competing with each other. The competition is fierce. Every group wants its piece of the American pie. Nowhere is this more evident than in the shaping of public school policy.

Christians wonder if they can be heard above the din. With so many others trying to put their ideas into policy, do Christians really stand a chance? Can Christian parents make any real difference in the public schools?

From the very first chapter of this book, I've been saying a loud "Yes!"

But if you've ever been involved with public education, you have experienced both "the thrill of victory and the agony of defeat." Schools will always be this way—there will be moments of keen disappointment along with the moments of great joy, as you try to change your school for the better. Educators try new programs. School boards experiment with new courses. Parents propose new ways to improve the social climate of their schools. Sometimes we succeed; we make constructive change. But there are still failures now and then: Misunderstanding between parents and school officials, upsets between students and teachers, and tense board meetings that bubble with hostile feelings.

Suppose you've gotten involved in the life of your local school. You've tried to bring a constructive change of some sort. And you've failed. What alternatives do you have? Well, you may think you have only three:

1. Fight the decision.
2. Admit defeat and sulk about it.
3. Pull your child out of the school.

But you have some other alternatives, too, and in this final chapter I'd like to explore some of them with you. I'd like to help you devise a *plan for action* that will insure that you can have a positive, Christian influence on your school.

The P.T.A. and S.A.C.

While the Parent-Teacher Association (P.T.A.) may be a good place to get involved in some schools, it is often only a fund-raising mechanism.

The national P.T.A. organization wants to wield influence over what happens in the daily operation of the school. In fact, they would like to have political power. The national P.T.A. has strong lobbyists in Congress. They are also interested in changing policies on the local level, through active P.T.A. chapters.

You are not likely to find a P.T.A. in many junior or senior high schools. This reflects disinterest on the part of the parents, on the part of the school officials, or both.

Some junior and senior high schools have School Advisory Councils. Such a group may include a representative from each academic area (i.e., an English teacher, a math teacher, etc.), a number of parents, some local business leaders, and the school principal. These councils make key decisions about school policy. They may be simply advisory groups; they may have the power to set official standards for the school. These councils must meet at intervals, not just when a crisis arises.

The principal might appoint members to the S.A.C. for a one-year term. They might meet each month for an hour-long discussion. Teachers, parents, and other interested persons may attend. So the S.A.C. gets input from all interested parties concerning a new idea; they have a chance to see whether it's "going to fly" in the community, before the school actually tries a new program. In this way, the S.A.C. can defuse potential powder kegs.

What Your Congregation Can Do

Now I realize that some churches urge their members to be completely separated from the public school system. They think the public schools are too "worldly." They believe the government is so corrupt that they can't afford to let their children be educated by a government agency.

But overall, churches are beginning to see that they must get involved in public education. They want to help their members influence school policy. Christians have a stake in the future of public education, because we cannot possibly send all of our children to private church-operated schools, nor should we. So church groups are trying to get on the front lines of action in their public schools. And that's what I'm encouraging you to do!

Your church can have a great impact on the future of

public education. You see, Christians are a potentially powerful and broadly-based group within our society. They have a strong base in nearly every urban and rural subunit of this nation. Nearly every voting precinct has at least one Christian congregation. Blacks, Hispanics, feminists, and other special-interest groups don't have that kind of representation.

The church of Jesus Christ stands in the midst of all the competing desires of the special-interest groups. Jesus said we are to be "the salt of the earth" (Matthew 5:13). We can be the world's most powerful force for moral and social change, if we will disperse ourselves into the world.

In past generations, Christians felt sure that all Americans had the same values we had. But that is not so. We are no longer culturally Christian. Other special-interest groups tout their unorthodox values as never before. In his insightful book entitled, *The Third Wave,* sociologist Alvin Toffler notes this trend. He says the American people "arrive at the workplace with an acute consciousness of their ethnic, religious, professional, sexual, subcultural, and individual differences. Groups that throughout the Second Wave era fought to be 'integrated' or 'assimilated' into mass society now refuse to melt their differences. They emphasize instead their unique characteristics."[1]

This new push for subgroup identity is a significant change in our society. But if any part of our society is able to adapt to change, it should be God's people. For we serve the God who never changes! Let's not be afraid to voice our convictions in the public arena. Let's not be ashamed to lift up our Christian standards. And let's not be afraid to talk face-to-face with people who have radically different standards—doing it with dignity and mutual respect.

Here are some specific projects your congregation might undertake, to impress your Christian convictions on public education:

Sponsor a Christian bookmobile. Outfit a van or an old bus with bookshelves and lights. Make it a bookroom on wheels! Then take it on a weekly route to parks, playgrounds, and any other area where children gather. This bookmobile ministry is especially effective in the summer. Fill it with inexpensive, wholesome books—paperbacks that you get from your Christian bookstore with donations from your own congregation.

Send flyers to the parents in the community you'll be visiting with the bookmobile. Put a little blurb in the newspaper, saying something like this: "On Tuesday mornings at 9:00 A.M., we'll park the First Christian bookmobile in the 300 block of North Maple. We have lots of good books for kids. Come and check out something to read." Be creative and think of other ways to publicize your bookmobile.

Not all parents are willing to take their children to a public library. In a small town or rural area, they might have to travel quite a distance to reach a public library. But your Christian bookmobile can bring good literature to their doorstep. It's a great way for you to minister to the children while they're out of school.

Set up a Christian summer school. Have you had a good response to your church's vacation Bible school? You probably have, especially if kids in your neighborhood have no other interesting activities to fill their summer months. Well, why not capitalize on that fact? Why not set up a Christian summer school, to meet for one or two months each year?

You'll find that the parents in your community will give strong support to a Christian summer school. The Community Church of Greenwood, Indiana has tried this with great success. They were disappointed with some of the things in their public school curriculum, and they'd not been able to change the curriculum. Instead of waging a war with the school officials, they started a Christian summer school. The minister,

Charles Lake, presented the program to his congregation by saying this:

Most of the youth in Community Church of Greenwood attend public schools. Community Church recognizes that the public schools do a good job of developing academic skills, providing valuable information, and educationally preparing our youth for the world in which they will live.

But most of the time, this educational experience is not put in the Christian perspective and, occasionally, may even be presented denouncing the Christian perspective. Each family individually and the church collectively have a responsibility to help our youth put their educational experience into a Christian perspective.

In order to carry out its responsibility in this matter, Community Church is proposing summer school classes which deal with the problem of assisting youth and their parents in relating public education to a Christian perspective. This is the primary aim of these summer school classes.[2]

They have a class called "God's Created World," for children who have finished the fifth grade. This course deals with evolution vs. creation, the Bible and recent findings of science, a Christian view of sexuality, and a Christian view of personal health and hygiene (drug education is part of this). They offer another class for students who have completed the sixth grade; it's called "God's Word to Live By." This is an overview of the entire Bible. It deals with the inspiration of Scripture, the themes of Scripture, the Bible as literature, the value of daily Bible study, and methods of personal Bible study. They offer a class on "God's Family Plan" for students who've finished the seventh grade. This provides a Biblical understanding of dating and marriage; of role models for husbands, wives, and children; divorce and its implications for family members; a plan for family worship; communication in marriage; sexual adjustments in marriage; and family finances. Finally, the church offers a course on "Godly Lifestyle" for those who've finished the eighth grade. This course tackles current social issues, secular humanism and its influence on modern morality, religious cults, basic Christian doctrines, and Christian moral standards of right and wrong.

These classes meet from 9:30 A.M. to 11:45 A.M. each day, five days a week. That gives the children about twelve hours of class time per week for four weeks.

The church charges $40 per student. The school runs throughout the month of June, and the church hires properly trained and certified Christian teachers for all the classes. It's an ambitious project! But your congregation could do something similar. It's practical. It's simple. And it doesn't require a large outlay of cash. (In fact, a Christian summer school usually pays for itself!)

Notice, too, that the Greenwood Church chose students at an ideal age for this type of program. Fifth graders are old enough to absorb a significant amount of new material in four weeks' time; but they're not old enough to have summer jobs which would interfere with the program. Kids at this age will be very responsive to Christian moral teaching.

Some school boards would even allow you to rent the public school facilities for a Christian summer school. By and large, the courts have held that if public schools make their facilities available to *any* community organization, they may not deny it to any organization. If the school board lets the Lions' Club use your school building on Tuesday nights, for example, they must allow your church to use the building at other times it is available.[3]

Support release-time religious education. Churches in

your area may already be sponsoring Weekday Religious Education (W.R.E.) or some other type of release-time program for the public schools. If so, you might consider joining this effort.

Release time works like this: A group of churches get the school board's permission to bring a trailer to the edge of the school property once a week, at a specified time. (Usually the school's club period works best.) The school agrees to release any of its students for that period to attend a religious class in the trailer. The churches provide the teacher, the trailer, and the curriculum; the school provides the time.

But there are problems with release time:

Some courts feel a release-time program violates the Constitution's separation of church and state. In 1979, the court in Chattanooga, Tennessee abolished a release-time Bible school for that reason.

Some release-time programs have been sued for personal injury when students were hurt in the trailer (which is not school property.)

There are ecclesiastical problems. Most W.R.E. or other release-time programs are sponsored by mainline denominational churches, which quite naturally want the teaching to reflect their liberal theology. So evangelical churches don't want to get involved. W.R.E. programs were started in the 1940s and 1950s in communities that had a heavy Roman Catholic or Lutheran population. These programs are on the decline now, and few evangelical churches want to sign on board a sinking ship! Especially when they feel uneasy about the curriculum.

If your community has W.R.E. or some other release-time program, check into it. See if it provides the kind of religious training you can approve. If it does, you might want to help sponsor it. There's no need for you to "reinvent the wheel," if someone else has already done it. But if your school doesn't have a release-time program already in place, I doubt that you can get one started. School officials are apt to say, "Well, you can have the children in church on Wednesday night and twice on Sunday. Why should we provide additional time for you to give religious instruction?"

Develop a Bible curriculum. If I could snap my fingers and instantly change anything in our public schools today, I'd like to see them start teaching the Bible as literature. I think our schools do a great disservice to their students by not teaching anything about the most popular book in the English language. (See my chapter on "Prayer and Bible Reading.") And your church can help to get this started.

You can band together with other churches in your community—churches from different doctrinal backgrounds—and draft a curriculum for teaching the Bible as literature, or choose one of the curriculums already marketed, a nonsectarian course in the Bible. Present this plan to your school board, saying, "Here's a course that doesn't try to win converts to any particular church. It won't offend anyone, no matter what their church background. And yet it gives our students a basic acquaintance with the Number One Book of all English literature." You might also identify other school districts in the area which have successfully implemented such a program. I think some school boards would be receptive to this kind of proposal.

Sponsor a scholarship for education students. I wonder what would happen to our public schools in the next ten years if churches began to view the schools as a mission field? I wonder what would happen if they put some of those resources toward training some dedicated Christian young people, who plan to teach in the public schools?

In other words, train missionaries for our schools!

I know a young man right now who is in his second year of public school teaching. He's a Christian. He and his wife turned down several offers from private Christian schools, because he felt he belonged in public school work. He waited and trusted the Lord for an opening there. He's now teaching fourth grade in a public school. His wife (a former student of mine) tells me that as soon as he completes his master's degree, he will go on to get his administrative license. He wants to be an elementary school principal. Imagine the tremendous impact this young man can make on our public schools! The same sort of thing can be done by any Christian young person who's called to the teaching profession.

What marvelous changes would come to our public schools if churches established scholarship funds to encourage Christian young people who want to be teachers! And school administrators! Ethel Herr says:

Many areas of our country are seeing massive teacher layoffs and program cutbacks caused by declining enrollments and slashed budgets. Educational careers offer unstable prospects in terms of job security. Teachers are being forced, either by low pay or by job cuts, to go into the world of industry in search of a livelihood. In such a climate, a young person with a teaching aptitude and interest needs all the encouragement we can give him.

When the outlook is so gloomy, why should we urge a child to pray and prepare for a career in education? Pat Patchen, executive secretary for the National Educators' Fellowship, suggests one good reason: "The need for Christians in the teaching profession has never been more urgent. As others are being advised to turn from the profession, why not urge Christian youth to enter it in a greater way than ever before? ... The future may call for fewer teachers, but it will always call for the best."[4]

Many churches already help to sponsor young people who are preparing for the ministry or foreign missions work. Why not do the same for young people who plan to work in the home mission field of the public schools? Here's how you can do it:

1. Adopt a formal policy statement, which views the public school system as a mission field.

2. Establish a scholarship fund to assist needy students who are majoring in education.

3. Set up a committee to be responsible for dispensing these funds.

4. Draw up a set of guidelines for dispensing these funds. Tell what qualifications the committee should seek in a scholarship student.

5. Develop a plan for securing these funds (i.e., by setting aside a percentage of your annual budget, by soliciting special gifts from wealthy individuals, by soliciting gifts from local corporations, etc.).

There's no denying that beginning teachers' salaries are low. Many students are not able to recoup the cost of getting a master's degree; they're not able to pay back their college loans. So they get discouraged and leave the teaching professions, as Mrs. Herr noted. Why not make it easier for Christian students to get that training? Why not encourage them to get into this vital field—and stay there?

If your congregation is not large enough to undertake this task alone, get together with another evangelical church in your area and set up a joint scholarship fund. You could select a committee from both congregations. And you could make the scholarship available to *any* Christian student in your community who meets the qualifications, not just to a student from your church.

There's Hope for the Future

When the missionary Hudson Taylor went to China to preach the gospel to people who were steeped in another religion, some of his friends despaired. They wondered why he would take on such a seemingly hopeless task. But Taylor replied, "The future is as bright as the promises of God!"

We need to remember that when we try to influence our public. Sure, the job seems hopeless at times. But remember Who gave us this assignment. The One who called you and me, as Christians, to be "the light of the world" was no less than the Lord of the world himself.

When we go into our schools with His love and concern in our hearts, the future is bright. When we set out to make the schools a place where our children can grow "in the nurture and admonition of the Lord," even as they grow in their knowledge of the world, the Lord goes with us. He leads us. He enables us to keep on trying to make our schools that kind of place.

"Lo, I am with you always, even to the end of the age," Jesus said (Matthew 28:20). He's with us in the school board meetings we attend. He's with us in our parent-teacher conferences. He's with us in the hallways where we tutor students, as school volunteers. Most important of all, He's with our students as they study in the public school classrooms day after day.

So we ought not to be cynical about the future of our schools. We ought to be hopeful. The Lord will be in their future, with us.

NOTES

[1]Alvin Toffler, *The Third Wave* (New York: Bantam Books, 1981), p. 232.

[2]"Community Church of Greenwood Christian Summer School," Greenwood Community Church, 1982, p. 1.

[3]The recent court decision concerning Christian clubs in the Lubbock, Texas schools casts a shadow on this policy. But I believe it will be reversed. See my chapter on "Prayer and Bible Reading."

[4]Ethel Herr, *Schools: How Parents Can Make a Difference* (Chicago: Moody Press, 1981), p. 158.

192